Dalit Politics and Literature

Dalit Politics and Literature

Pradeep K. Sharma

SHIPRA

First Published in India 2006

Rs. 650; US$ 32.50

ISBN: 978-81-7541-598-0

2011 Edition

Dalit Politics and Literature

Published by:
SHIPRA PUBLICATIONS
H.O.: LG-18-19, Pankaj Central Market,
Patparganj, I.P. Ext., Delhi 110092,
Ph. 91-11-2223 5152, 2223 6152
Br. Off.: 4617/18, Ansari Road, Delhi 110002;
Ph. 91-11-6594 6453, 9810522367

Email: info@shiprapublications.com
Website: www.shiprapublications.com

Preface

The Dalit movements in India have occupied significant place in the history of social movements as well as in the discourse of social sciences. These movements have undergone several phases, particularly during the twentieth century, right from its struggles for recognition, mobilization, co-option, power sharing to cultural and literary assertions as well as identity assertions through variety of methods and strategies, which covers effectively every aspect of human life. The broad canvas of the Dalit movements encompasses multiple tiers of long and painful struggles for universal values of equality, democratization, freedom, human dignity, solidarity and radical transformation of society that could ensure a dignified human existence. These movements have addressed numerous issues that facilitate to understand and analyse Indian polity, especially post-Independence, in a more objective and comprehensive manner. In terms of strategy and methods, these movements have also witnessed wide range from grassroots activism to alliance building and also to international networking and global solidarity. These sustained and continued struggles make Dalit movements not only inspiring but also the living movements of the contemporary times.

It is this untiring struggle and universal appeal of the movements that motivates me to work on the different aspects of the Dalit movements in India in general and North India in particular. This book is the outcome of my more than eight years of engagement with the subject as researcher and is the revised version of my doctoral thesis from the Jawaharlal Nehru University, New Delhi, India.

The literary expression of political consciousness and movements among or for the Dalits in North India is the new emerging trend. Though, we find instances of such protest expressions even during the colonial period, it is a recent phenomenon in this region that has established Hindi Dalit Literature as the protest literature that contributes to the movements and the cause. The Hindi Dalit Literature is not a 'leisure' or 'elitist' literature but literature of the people, of oppressed and marginalized. This trend has served enormously to the cause and also is able to widen its constituency in different regards; political and intellectual as well as local, regional, national and global. Here, the scenario is bit complex where political mobilisation is conjoined with cultural and literary identity and is expressed through variety of forms, either drama, novel, autobiography, memoir, poetry or reportage. It is also interface with the 'mainstream literature', questioning its hierarchies, hegemonic sophistication both in form and content and endeavouring for notions and theories of aesthetics of the oppressed and marginalized. It is important to reiterate that the cultural and literary identities crystallise with on-going political mobilisation and sometimes, play the role of lighthouse and torchbearers in the course of movements for empowerment. This is precisely the task that Hindi Dalit Literature is performing in this region, more vocally since 1990s onwards.

The book explores this relationship between politics and literature with a critical analysis of eleven texts from the Hindi literature both by Dalits and non-Dalits. This task is not only explorative but challenging as well. An attempt is being made to underline not only the major issues and concerns of the movements but also to demonstrate that political consciousness is also expressed through many more innovative and creative methods like art and literature and not only through conventional means all the times.

Many people have inspired and supported me in this endeavour and I humbly thank all of them, in particular to the renowned faculty members of the Centre for Political Studies, Jawaharlal Nehru University, who were always generous in shaping my queries and knowledge and extended invaluable suggestions. They were always very supportive throughout the course of this work.

Special thanks are due to Professor Kiran Saxena, my research supervisor, Professor Balvir Arora, Professor Zoya Hasan, Professor Gurpreet Mahajan, Professor Rakesh Gupta, Professor Valerian Rodrigues, Professor Gopal Guru, Dr. Shefali Jha, Dr. Vidhu Verma, Dr. Pralay Kanungo, Dr. Asha Sarangi, Dr. Rahul Mukherji and Dr. T.G. Suresh. I am also thankful to all those scholars, from different centres of JNU, who provided me all help during the course of this work notable Professor Nandu Ram, Professor Anand Kumar, Dr. Vivek Kumar, Professor Manager Pandey, Dr. Devendra Choubey and Professor Kanti Bajpai, who is now in Doons.

Professor C.P. Bhambri, Professor Kuldeep Mathur, Professor Sudha Pai, and Professor Niraja Gopal Jayal have been constant source of motivation and I express my deep gratitude to all of them with utmost sincerity and humility.

Further my thanks are due to Professor Harmeet Singh Uppal who not only sent me relevant material regarding contemporary Dalit discourse but also helped me to more about Panjab and Madya Pradesh politics and their literary expressions. He also helped me to analyse *Dharti Dhan Na Apana* by Jagdish Chandra that is contextualized in Punjab.

I also wish to thank Werner Welschoff, my German friend, for his curious discussions from time to time about the progress of this book and also sometimes, his innocent queries about Indian politics that led me to shape some of my ideas during the course of this work. Thanks to Rajesh Paswan for his support and wishes.

I am also thankful to Shipra Publications and particularly to Mr. Kumar for his support and encouragement and timely completion of the book.

There is another acknowledgement, which I desire to make with more confidence, love and greetings. It is an acknowledgement of debt that I owe to Disha Uppal who remains to be a witness of my struggling life and endeavoured to be a friend and companion. She not only encouraged me to think by her presence but also consistently motivated me, by her questions, to revise and correct my thoughts. Thanking her for all efforts, she has put in for successful completion of this book would remain wordless due to the limitation of written expressions.

Important to mention that any omission and mistakes are my responsibility and I humbly accept that for further improvements.

Finally, I owe an immense debt of gratitude to my parents and family members who have always inspired me to be optimistic even during the darkest hour of my life. I don't know how to express my gratitude to my late Amma, without whom I feel so disenchanted for life and I know that I am able to complete this work because I have her and her blessings on my side. She always taught me to believe in the optimism of will and I wish she could have seen this book during her lifetime, but alas!

October 2005 **Pradeep K. Sharma**

Contents

Preface v

1. **Introduction** 1

2. **Political Consciousness and Literary Expression** 13

   Literary Expression / 20; Idealism / 23; Positivism / 27; Formalism / 29; Structuralism / 31; Sociological Literary Criticism / 33; Marxist School / 35; Placing Hindi Dalit Literature / 43

3. **Dalit Consciousness and Movement** 52

   Meaning of the term 'Movement' / 57; Brief History of Dalit Movement / 61; Dalit Literature and Aesthetics / 78

4. **Premchand to Mannu Bhandari: Critical Analysis** 83

   Kafan (1936): Premchand / 88; Godan (1936): Premchand / 92; Dharati Dhan Na Apana (1972): Jagdish Chandra / 103; Nachyo Bahut Gopal (1978): Amrit Lal Nagar / 108; Mahabhoj (1979): Mannu Bhandari / 113

5. **Mohan Dass Naimishray to Recent Writings Towards Empowerment** 121

   Apne Apne Pinjare (1995): Mohan Dass Naimishray / 123; Socio-economic Context / 123; Cultural Context / 125; Political Context/126; Kranti Shesh Hai (1995): Lalchand 'Rahi' / 129; Suno Brahaman (1996): Malkhan Singh / 131; Joothan (1997): Om Prakash Balmiki / 133; Socio-political Context / 134; Gunga Nahin Tha Main (1997): Jai Prakash Kardam / 139; Harry Kab Aayega (1999): Suraj Pal Chauhan / 140

6. Dalit Politics and Literature: Future Trends **144**

Annexure 162

Bibliography 165

Index 174

1

Introduction

Indian society is divided into numerous castes and sub-castes, numbering roughly over four thousand; besides a sizeable number of tribes and other religious communities. Castes have come out of ancient fourfold classification of society known as '*Varna*'. There are four *Varnas*: (*i*) *Brahmins* who were supposed to be the priests and custodians of knowledge; (*ii*) *Kshatriyas* who were expected to be the rulers and soldiers; (*iii*) *Vaishyas* who were traders and landholders; (*iv*) *Shudras* who provide other needed services. A fifth group, the *Panchamas* is put at the lowest rung and performed menial and despicable services. They were considered external to the system and, subsequently, are known by several nomenclatures, *e.g.*, *Harijan*, the Scheduled Castes (SCs) and the *Dalits*.

G.S. Ghurye[1] has earmarked six classical features of Indian Caste System, *viz.*, segmental divisions of society based on birth; a definite scheme of social hierarchy; restrictions of feeding and social intercourse; civil and religious disabilities; lack of unrestricted choice of occupation and restriction on marriages. This Caste System puts *Brahmins* at the top and *Shudra* at the bottom with a sizeable population outside the *Varna* scheme known as the Untouchables.

The Untouchable or the *Dalits*, as they are presently known, are one of the most vulnerable sections of society in our country. They constitute nearly 17 percent (over 13 crores) of the total population in the country but have been subjected to multiple for oppression and subjugation for centuries and had lived miserable life as Mukundrao Patil, a major figure in the Maharashtrian anti-caste Stayashodhak Samaj, writes "India is a strange place, which collects all sorts of social groups, divided by different religions, thoughts, practices and understandings. But broadly speaking, they can be categorized into two: the majority low castes that have been devoid of humanity for centuries and a handful who take their pleasure, call themselves superior and live at the cost of the majority. One's welfare is another's misery; that is their connection."[2]

In this way, "majority" was made 'Untouchable' section of the society and was called by different nomenclature from time to time like *'Harijan'* 'Scheduled Castes' (SCs) and *'Dalit'*. The term '*Dalit*' has a wide connotation and is a self-chosen: one that is very much prevalent in the contemporary times. The *Dalit* Panthers in 1972-73 widened the meaning of the term *Dalit* when they incorporated various religions minorities, women, tribals, backward castes and economically deprived sections in their definition.[3] Today, many social scientists have started referring to the *Dalits*, inter-changeably as untouchables or the SCs. The proposed work also uses the term *Dalit* for ex-untouchables or SCs who are articulating their self-realization and their struggle against the caste-oppression; their "will to act against exploitation, a 'determined' rise from oppression, from death to life, from darkness to light"[4] and continuing their movement.

The second definitional perspective is regarding the meaning and nature of political consciousness, with special reference to the *Dalits*. Political consciousness implies one's self-image *vis-à-vis* other social communities, individual's relations with socio-political location and his/her connectivity with socio-politico-economic structures of the society. Political consciousness characterizes a community's cognitive comprehensibility of its objective conditions whose subjective awareness is formed through social experiences, political struggles and cultural traits.

Political consciousness is generally not a homogeneous category in nature and functions but has various levels of latent and manifest expressions operating within it, which are influenced by the complexity of the social structures. In fact, the dialectical relationship between immediate achievements and long-term impact on the whole society can be located in various levels of political consciousness, thus making it a fundamental feature of human existence; possessing not only self awareness but, even more, a remarkable capacity to understand what is happening how, when and where.

Clubbed with political participation, which is not confined to a relatively limited sets of acts such as voting, campaigning or participation through a very formal institutionalised behaviour but which refers to "any voluntary action, successful or unsuccessful, organized of unorganised, episodic or continuous, employing legitimate or illegitimate methods, intended in influencing the choice of public affairs and policies, the administration of public works of the choice of political leaders",[5] political consciousness becomes 'a functional catalyst' providing general participation orientations, community mobilization and identity building processes.

Thus understood, political consciousness becomes an instrumental tool for any community to articulate their orientations, identity building processes, mobilization strategies and others aspects of their movements. Accordingly, the *Dalit* community has shaped themselves for a 'new self-image' starting roughly from the *Bhakti* Movement (12th to 18th centuries) which attempted to purify Hinduism of its evils and fought against the tyranny of the caste system and produced great saints like Chokhamela, Eknath, Pandita Ramabai, Kabir, Ravidas and many more who left an immense appeal for the establishment of an egalitarian society. Later on, Mahatma Jotiba Phule paid emphasis on educational, social and political development of the community which was, finally, articulated by Dr. B.R. Ambedkar who "played three roles: that of a caste leader, that of an Untouchable spokesman, and that of a national statesman"[6] He formed three political parties (Independent Labour Party, Scheduled Castes Federation and the Republican Party of India) preparing ground for the *Dalit* Panthers and other similar formations of the community which were performing task of the proliferation of the political consciousness at various levels from understanding of the self to the transformation of society with a visionary movement. We will analyse the brief history of the *Dalit* movement in India, including Dr. Ambedkar's contribution, in Chapter Three of this study.

Political consciousness is expressed through various means including the literary expression. This study starts by accepting the possibility of a close interaction and relationships between politics, literary and creative expressions. Besides, it gains impetus from recognition of the necessity to understand the nature of this relationship in concrete situation to have a holistic understanding of true nature of some social and political movements, in particular, the *Dalit* movement, in contemporary India.

The significance of relationship between politics and literary expression can be objectively defined only when we take a comprehensive view of social reality around us that comprises of what we classify as the political, social, economic, cultural and ideological aspects of a social reality. It is necessary to examine and investigate social reality with a comprehensive approach analysing all aspects of particular phenomenon and their mutual interaction and significance.

By accepting this possibility of a close relationship between politics and creative literature, this study tends to recognize the nature, extend, depth and impact of this relationship in the objective situations to have a holistic understanding of the *Dalit* movement in contemporary Indian society. The first question, in this direction, is that of defining literature and literary expression.

The general assumption of this study is straightforward that all writers, great or minor ones, are confronted with political issues of their times in their works. Either they draw inspiration from any political development of their period or their works have left an important impact on the course of the political issues. This impact is more important in case of the political literature like the *Dalit* literature where *Dalits*, by the very nature of their movement, choose to deny hegemony of the caste order and its various justifications.

Literature is neither a static collection of written expressions authored by a writer nor documentation. Rather it is ever-evolving and developing, keeping tune with the changing times. Literature and its concepts are deeply associated with the development and progress of society. It is basically the development of the heart of the people and a cherished, assetful accumulation of knowledge of a particular time period reflecting society in a mirroristic way.[7] Literature becomes a chastened reflection of the feelings of the masses along with the social relation weaved with the literary imagination by a writer.

There are various schools of literature and its sociology, for instance, the Positivism, Formalism, Empiricism and Structuralism; where each school of thought has a particular opinion about literature and its sociology. Empiricists regard literature as a social fact, which possesses no definite element, meaning or nature but is an integral part of the storehouse of knowledge and its Mata narratives. One has to understand the specific and objective situations of social phenomenon to get a holistic view of literature that lays emphasis on a close interaction and inter relationship between the author, his/her works and the readers.

This relationship prompts us to examine various socio-eco-political, aesthetics, psychological and ethical aspects of the author, his/her works and the readers, along with the objective conditions. Some scholars are of the opinion that socio-political institutions also play vital role in the development of literature and insist on their study, importance and significance.

Another set of scholars consider literature as a social activity affected by the changing nature of the society while Marxists view literature as a social product in a capitalistic society which reflect the conditions of production, marketing and consumption, also, becoming a historical evidence, possibly, developing the social consciousness.

There are various schools of thought for the study of the sociology of literature *e.g.*, Positivist (Hippolyte, Adolph, Taine); Formalism (Victor Shklovski); Structuralism (Lucien Goldmann); Sociological Literary Criticism (Leo Lowenthal); and Marxists (Georg Luckas, Raymond Williams). We'll discuss these schools in Chapter Two of this study.

Thus analysed, literature can be said a chastened accumulation of knowledge represented by an author through various mediums of written/unwritten expressions narrating feelings, experiences, ethos of a particular social actor or phenomenon which may be affected by the complexities of a given socio-political and cultural system or may be affected vice versa. Political literature is a loaded category and we'll examine existing The Hindi *Dalit* Literature in this perspective.

Thus seen, literary expression is a creative exercise to transform social reality into various mediums of expression which works as an analysing framework for socio-political and cultural phenomena and becomes a treasured repository of knowledge. This expression differs and varies in degree, intensity, scope and success from author to author and with one author from work to work. But different ways of expressions, to translate political development into literary texts with political and creative imagination, comprehend their ability to harness and demonstrate the social development and to produce masterpiece political literature. Some times we find a serious coherence coming out of various political viewpoints and also a mutual connection between literature and political ideas, debates and issues.

To identify and sketch out a theoretical framework, for the study of close interaction between politics and literature, is a challenging task examining different viewpoints about this relationship where some denounce such a thing while other emphasis political role and its importance in literary expression. We'll analyse, in subsequent chapters, particularly in chapter two, this role focussing mainly on the Idealist (Benedetto Croce), Positivist (Taine), Formalist (Shklovski), Structuralist (Goldmann), Sociological Literary Criticism (Lowenthal) and Marxists (Lukacs, Raymond Williams) standpoints, thus, exploring a theoretical narrative.

This work primarily focuses on the literary expression of political consciousness among the *Dalits*, largely in the northern region of the country. We find a rich variety of Hindi *Dalit* Literature in the area that it becomes crucial to make a selection from such a vast variety of literary expressions. Hindi region has several specificities in terms of the *Dalit* politics and literature. First of all, the ideals of Dr. Ambedkar started influencing the course of the *Dalit* movement in this region only during early-1950s. We also notice influence of Mahatma Gandhi on the politics and anti-colonial struggle in this region. This factor shaped not only the political but also literary expression of this region. Hence, it is important to understand all these factors to get a holistic view of politics and literature in the Hindi region.

Placing Hindi *Dalit* literature[8] amidst these theoretical narratives is not only necessary but is also urgently required as to understand, analyse, address and highlight socio-cultural and politico-economic dynamics of the *Dalit* community. The *Dalit* literature, primarily, narrates first hand experience of the community; aiming to make aware of multiple oppressions and also to protest/revolt against domination of the upper castes in Indian society. *Dalit* writers believe that literature needs to be interpreted/narrated or written sociologically and *Dalit* literature must be interpreted not only as a piece of artistic work but more as representation of that time and those situations faced by the community which are being narrated by the writer.

Of course, this perspective is placed in altogether different

Weltanschauung and demands realistic, empirical and authentic notions of aesthetics which may be called as the *Dalit* aesthetics. Here, *Dalit* writers negate traditional notions of literary aesthetics and experience the need for the construction of new aesthetics that could capture their problems, torture and pain faced and experienced by the individual or community. This notion of aesthetics puts 'man' at the centre of narration and analysis aspiring for equality, freedom, justice and solidarity for the whole of humanity. We would examine Hindi *Dalit* Literature with this perspective in subsequent chapters, especially in Chapter Three.

It is important to understand the very meaning and nature of the Hindi *Dalit* Literature. Hindi *Dalit* Literature is, in fact, political literature due to its in-built denial of hegemony of the Indian Caste System and its inspiration drawn from the *Dalit* Movement. *Dalit* Literature considers man as its centre and depicts trauma, pain, exploitation and suppression of the community in a very creative and lucid expressive ways. To understand the *Dalit* Literature requires in-depth sociological analysis of the community, its protests, its self-articulations and movements. This study, in the subsequent chapters, explores the nature and depth of these aspects related to the *Dalit* movement and attempts to associate it with the *Dalit* aesthetics and narratives.

It is to be noted here that this kind of understanding regarding interaction between literary expression and political consciousness facilitates in presenting a complete picture of any movement, its ideological, socio-economic, politico-cultural basis and provide a comprehensive narrative.

This study is exploratory in nature and emphasizes on the qualitative framework of analysis. To understand level of political consciousness among the Dalits through literary expression is not an easy task, if not an impossible one, and it remains complex and challenging. Primarily, this study makes an effort to search for a theoretical basis of relationship and interaction between politics and literary expressions from the socio-politico-ideological viewpoints. In this context, it explores to investigate various theoretical debates, viz. the Idealist, Positivist, Liberal and Marxist.

The study endeavours to explore extent and depth of literary expressions in the Hindi *Dalit* Literature spreading through various time spans. Hence, it proposes to study various noted figures of Hindi literature like Munshi Premchand, Jagdish Chandra, Amrit Lal Nagar, Mannu Bhandari, Mohan Dass Naimishray, Om Prakash Balmiki, Malkhan Singh, Jai Prakash Kardam, Lalchand *'Rahi'* and Suraj Pal Chauhan. This has provided an opportunity to encompass a wide range of the twentieth century that covers the Ambedkar period and comes down to the contemporary *Dalit* movement in the country.

This study has made an attempt to cover major time spans of the twentieth century as expressed through a juxtaposed and complex relationship between literary expression and level of political participation among the *Dalits*. Historically and intellectually, it assesses various aspects related to this subject like literature and protest, literature and communicative dimensions in the extent of the work.

Three kinds of literary studies have been critically examined in the course of this study:

(*a*) Studies identified as classics of their age in the backdrop of their socio-historical conditions; (Representative studies).

(*b*) Studies identifying aspects of literary expressions and their structures in relation to the parallel social systems in which they originate and thereby their impact as well; (Form-based studies)

(*c*) Studies identifying tendencies of literature that can be seen over a range of several works and thereby place them in their socio-political origin (Studies narrating trends)

Objectives and Rationale

1. Political consciousness is expressed through various means; literary expression is one of them, hence, to assess and examine their relationship.
2. To discuss various ideological debates on the sociology of literature and placing the Hindi *Dalit* Literature in a perspective.
3. To investigate socio-political contexts represented in the Hindi *Dalit* Literature.
4. To understand the processes shaping the consciousness of

the *Dalits* in specific socio-political conditions.

5. To understand the nature of representation of the *Dalits* in Hindi Literature.
6. To examine how political consciousness affects the *Dalit* aesthetics in Hindi Literature.
7. To explore the possibility for a theoretical narrative of *Dalit* politics and literature.

The Ecological Model of Research primarily guides this study that consists four concentric circles. The first one deals with the individual actor, his personality and behavioural traits; the second one represents immediate context in which that actor is placed; the third one represents formal/informal institutions of social structures and their relationship with the actor and the fourth one investigates social, economic and cultural environment. In this way, a comprehensive effort has been made to explore and understand the social reality operating at different tiers of social, political and cultural levels.[9]

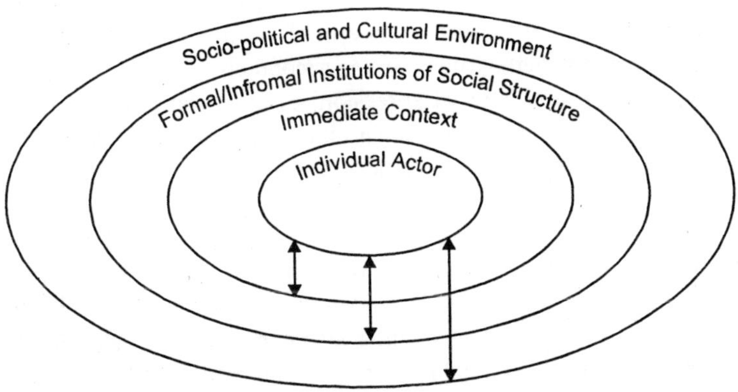

This endeavour requires both primary and secondary sources. As this study is concentrated on political consciousness among the *Dalits*, authoritative works on the *Dalit* Movement and politics in India were consulted. To examine literary expressions, wide range of literary works in Hindi literature were consulted, particularly the *Dalit* literature so as to ascertain relationship between political consciousness, literary expression and the *Dalit* aesthetics. Apart from the major texts, critiques and other literary summaries are also being analysed in the course of this study. Major texts are:

1. *Godan* (1936, Novel): Premchand
2. *Kafan* (1936, Story): Premchand
3. *Dharati Dhan Na Apana* (1972, Novel): Jagdish Chandra
4. *Nachyo Bahut Gopal* (1978, Novel-cum-Reportage): Amrit Lal Nagar
5. *Maha Bhoj* (1979, Novel): Mannu Bhandari
6. *Apne Apne Pinjare* (1995, Autobiography): Mohandass Naimishray
7. *Kranti Shesh Hai* (1995, Poetry): Lalchand *'Rahi'*
8. *Suno Brahaman* (1996, Poetry): Malkhan Singh
9. *Joothan* (1997, Autobiography): Om Prakash Balmiki
10. *Gunga Nahin Tha Main* (1997, Poetry): Jai Prakash Kardam
11. *Harry Kab Aayega* (1999, Short Stories): Suraj Pal Chauhan.

The study has been divided into six chapters. In this first chapter, which is **Introductory**, we have already dealt with a brief analysis of the problem, its nature, conceptual framework, definitional perspectives and methodology. In the second chapter titled 'Political Consciousness and Literary Expression' an endeavour has been made to define the meaning and nature of political consciousness. Ideological debates on political consciousness and interplay of politics and literature have been dealt extensively in this chapter. Challenging task of defining literary expression, its relationship with political consciousness, debates pertaining to the interaction between creative literature and politics has been undertaken exhaustively during the course of this chapter. This chapter also explores influence, impact and implications of political movements on literature and vice-versa, and attempts to search for a theoretical narrative. The third chapter titled '*Dalit* Consciousness Movement' deals with the meaning and nature of the term *Dalit* consciousness including the word *Dalit*, meaning of the term 'movement', a brief history of the *Dalit* Movement in India, *Dalit* Literature and *Dalit* Aesthetics, influence of *Dalit* Movement on the *Dalit* Literature. Chapter fourth titled 'Premchand to Mannu Bhandari Critical Analysis' examines critically selected works of Hindi littérateurs like *Godan*, Kafan (Premchand); *Dharati Dhan Na Apana* (Jagdish Chandra); *Nachyo Bahut Gopal* (Amrit Lal Nagar); Maha Bhoj (Mannu Bhandari). In this chapter, critical analysis has been made to understand Hindi Dalit literature as presented by the non-Dalit writers and its very importance to the major discourse of entitlement. Chapter five titled 'Mohan Dass Naimishray to recent writings Towards Empowerment' like *Apne Apne Pinjare* (Mohandas Naimishray); *Kranti Shesh Hai* (Lalchand *'Rahi'*); *Suno Brahaman* (Malkhan Singh); *Joothan* (Om Prakash Balmiki); *Gunga Nahin Tha Main* (Jai Prakash Kardam) and *Harry Kab Aayega* (Suraj Pal Chauhan). This chapter deals comprehensively with all the selected texts and examines prevalent political and literary streams in those texts. We have attempted to provide a critical analysis of all the works so as to have a holistic view of literature and politics. An attempt is made in chapter six titled '*Dalit* Politics and Literature: Future Trends' to construct a theoretical narrative of the *Dalit* politics and literature. In this chapter, we have dealt with the Durban Process and the Bhopal Conference and Declaration to highlight the contemporary issue before the *Dalit* politics and also analysed briefly some of the views on the issue of aesthetics for the Hindi *Dalit* Literature.

NOTES

1. Ghurye, G.S. *Caste and Race in India* (Bombay: Popular Prakashan, 1932).
2. Patil, Mukundrao Din Mitra, June 1913; cited in Gail Omvedt, *Cultural Revolt in a Colonial Society: The Non-Brahaman Movement in Western India 1873-1930* (Pune: Scientific Socialist Education Trust, 1976) p. 157.
3. Manifesto of the *Dalit* Panthers, 1972.
4. Omvedt, Gail. *Dalit and Democratic Revolution: Dr. Ambedkar and the Dalit Movement in Colonial India* (Delhi: Sage Publications, 1994) p. 11.
5. Weiner, Myron. *'Political Participation: Crisis of the Political Process'*, in L. Binder, *et al*,. (eds) *Crisis and Sequences in Political Development* (Princeton: Princeton University Press, 1979) p. 164.
6. Zelliot, Eleanor. *From Untouchable to Dalit: Essays on the Ambedkar Movement*, (Delhi: Manohar Publishers & Distributors, 1992) p. 53.
7. Various books and texts on the meaning and nature of literature and its sociology have been consulted to arrive at a working definition of literature. Several debates around these issues are discussed in the subsequent chapters.
8. Defining Hindi *Dalit* Literature is a difficult task. There are two major line

of arguments: one advocates that only that literature could be termed as *Dalit* Literature which is being written by the *Dalit* authors (because only they can express authentic picture of the trauma and exploitation) while another line of argument advocates that even if an upper caste author is writing that could depicts authentic picture of the *Dalit* community then his/her work could be termed as a part of the *Dalit* Literature. This study has focused on both kinds of work and analyzes works of Munshi Premchand, Mannu Bhandari, Amrit Lal Nagar, Om Prakash Balmiki and Mohandas Naimishray.

9. Both primary and secondary texts were consulted for methodology; major texts are Partha Nath Mukherji (ed.), *Methodology in Social Research* (Delhi: Sage Publications, 2000); Ranjit Kumar. *Research Methodology* (London: Sage Publications, 1999); Pauline V. Young. *Scientific Social Surveys and Research* (Delhi: Prentice-Hall of India, 1992). Ecological model is being considered most feasible to understand, examine and analyse the nature and scope of the subject where a close correlation between political consciousness and literary expression could be properly understood.

2

Political Consciousness and Literary Expression

Definition of a notion, term or idea itself is a very complex process. The term 'definition' means describing exactly the characteristics, nature, scope, dynamics and limitations with utmost possible clarity and precision about a particular phenomenon. In this way, research definition should be a systematic investigation into and study of materials and sources in order to establish facts to reach new and valid conclusions. The process of obtaining a research definition involves careful, systematic, patient study and investigation establishing reliable and valid knowledge about the social world around us.

The definition of a concept as complex as political consciousness would necessarily incorporate examination of socio-eco-political and cultural processes operating in the society and as this study is guided by the Ecological Model, it would also examine political consciousness spread over different levels: individual, family, community and state as dispersed in several functional domains of social and political interactions.

Political consciousness constitutes knowledge about political institutions, its dynamics and processes and is a key concept for understanding the political system. It has strong correlation with participatory orientation and political efficiency of the people. The level of political consciousness has far-reaching consequences for successful functioning of democracy because if people are well informed about political issues, they will participate more meaningfully in political processes and take enlightened decisions. In fact, possession of minimum level of political consciousness leads to certain degree of involved political participation. Political consciousness is constitutive and relational in its nature and content where the constitutive elements represent political comprehension of feelings, thoughts, beliefs, idea, experiences, awareness and cognitions (both subjective and objective) and the relational element establish connections between individual's understanding of the self (that subsequently becomes the political self) and the relation with external world.

This makes the concept of political consciousness complex one to define; and its analysis involves processes of its formation, articulation, expression and manifestations both at the subjective and objective levels. The concept is not monolithic and homogenous but incorporates several tiers particularly in a heterogeneous and multi-cultural society like India. Indian society comprises of numerous castes and sub-castes numbering roughly around over four thousand besides the sizeable number of tribes and other religious communities. Other than the castes, Indian society is characterised with colonial legacy, developing political institutions that are not very established one and fragile political culture. To understand political consciousness in this kind of socio-political set up becomes quite complex and intricate which requires critical examination of all issues around this concept.

Political consciousness implies one's self-image *vis-à-vis* other individual and social communities; their relationship with socio-political locations and their linkages/connectivity with socio-eco-political and cultural structures of society. Political consciousness characterises a community's cognitive comprehensibility of its objective conditions as well as its subjective awareness that, in turn, is formed through social experiences, political struggles and cultural traits.

Political consciousness is not a homogeneous category in nature and function but has various levels of latent and manifest expression operating within it, which are influenced by the complexities of social structures. In fact, the dialectical relationship between immediate achievements and long-term impact on the whole society can be located in various levels of political consciousness thus making it a "functional feature of human existence"[1] possessing not only self-awareness but even more a remarkable capacity to understand what is happening, when where and how.

In this way, political consciousness signifies a continuous

process that, possibly, begins from cradle and continues till grave. In its wider connotation, it includes processes like political socialisation, political modernisation, political culture and political development. In fact, political consciousness is an understanding of the entire socio-political system that affects the development and progress of one's life at every level: individual, familial, communitarian, state and socio-cultural.

Before exploring a working definition for political consciousness, it is important to understand certain concepts and terms like political and politics, processes like political socialisation, political culture, political modernisation, political development and political system and their meaning, nature and scope as clarity of these concepts and processes would provide insights and impetus to find out a comprehensive working definition for political consciousness.

The term 'politics' is derived from the Greek words: *'polis'* and *'politeia'* which embraces everything that touches life of an individual and the state. Greeks were having an organic view of politics which became a trilogy for them incorporating theory of the State, theory of the Morals and theory of Law. Politics was understood as "the distilled wisdom of the age"[2] and a political man possessed insatiable curiosity to know the unknown fact; a scientific attitude and instinct for criticism wielded by Reason; debated the concept of Idea and Form and they had a very dynamic Theory of Justice.

Subsequent philosophers and writers contributed to the development of the term and broadly distinguished between theoretical politics and applied politics. Theoretical politics included:

1. Theory of the State;
2. Theory of the Government;
3. Theory of Legislation; and
4. Theory of the State as an artificial person.

While the applied or practical politics included:

1. The State (actual forms of government);
2. The Government (working of government, administration and other);
3. Laws and Legislation (courts, procedures etc.); and

4. State personified (diplomacy, peace, war and international relations).

This understanding of the terms politics and political expanded the horizon and encompasses virtually every sphere of human activity and life within its orbit. The dynamics of the term politics has three connotations[3]:

1. Politics as a political activity;
2. Politics as a political process; and
3. Politics as political power.

Oakeshott defines political activity as "an activity in which human beings related to one other as members of a civil association, think and speak about the arrangements and the conditions of their association from the point of view of their desirability, make proposals about changes in these arrangements and condition, try to persuade others of the desirability of the proposed changes and act in such a manner as to promote the changes"[4]. He further elaborates "in political activity, then, men sail a boundless and bottomless sea; there is neither harbour for shelter nor floor for anchorage; neither starting place nor appointed destination. The enterprise is to keep afloat on an even keel; the sea is both friend and enemy"[5]

Political process is an extension of the sense of political activity that includes the study of the dynamics of political and civil association, socio-psychological analysis of actors who are operationalising their ideas affecting the very nature of political activity. It is a continuous process and is shaped by several factors.

Political power is "the capacity of an individual, or a group of individuals, to modify the conduct of other individuals or groups in the manner which he desires"[6] Robert Dahl explains power in a very succinct way: "A has power over B to the extent he can get B to do something that B would not otherwise do"[7]. The concept of political power embraces the entire gambit of political system and political power when exercised with legitimacy becomes constitutional responsibility while without legitimacy and constitutional propriety, it remains as manifestation of brute force. A critical investigation of politics examines description and analysis of the ways power is obtained, exercised and controlled, the purpose for which it is used, the dynamics of decision-making and the factors and contexts in which those decisions are made and executed.

Thus examined, the concept of politics has comprehensive meaning and possesses complex nature with wide scope. It includes, on the one hand, the study of its theoretical formulations and narratives whereas on the other, it critically scrutinises the applied and empirical factors affecting the very nature of body politic. It takes into account all spheres of political activity, political process and political power. It is one of the most dynamic and ever-evolving concepts of human activities and the very meaning, nature and scope of the term–politics, determine different tiers of political consciousness. A politically conscious person, however fluid in character, would possess a sense of political activity, political process and political power. We would examine, in subsequent chapters, how this understanding of political consciousness is pertinent and important for the analysis of the *Dalit* consciousness and movement.

Another process deeply associated with political consciousness is that of political socialisation. Political socialisation "is the process by which political cultures are maintained and changed. Through the performance of this function, individuals are inducted into the political culture and their orientations towards political objects are formed"[8]. It is a learning process where gradual learning occurs for the norms, attitudes and behaviours acceptable to the contemporary political system. Applied in narrow sense, this concept may appear conservative and status-quoist but if it is adoptable with an understanding for the study of change, it may provide substantial empirical data, particularly for analysis as it would include different stages of political socialisation, *i.e.*, childhood, adolescence, youth, adulthood and old age, and also, several agents of political socialisation like family, peers, friends, institutions, political parties and associations and state.

The quality of this concept lies in the fact that it is a process that makes detailed analytical instrument for the study of any social phenomena. The analysis of processes of political socialisation becomes unavoidable for a critical study of political consciousness among *Dalits* because it would address the multiple processes leading towards the formation of political consciousness of an individual and community. It would examine politics of protest, its feasibility and viability, its limitations and experiences of success and failures. Investigations would further incorporate the transmission of political knowledge from one generation to another and its operationalisation with several variants. Hence, political consciousness is also analysed with socialisation processes and its limitations.

Thus, a comprehensive understanding of political consciousness would include the study of politics, processes of political socialisation and political culture, its impact on the construction of political consciousness among the *Dalits* and its different ways of expression in the Hindi *Dalit* Literature.

Analysed in this way, the most powerful component of political consciousness becomes political participation and expression. Political participation is not confined to a relatively limited sets of acts such as voting, campaigning or participation through a very formal institutionalised behaviour but refers to "any voluntary action, successful or unsuccessful, organised or unorganised, episodic or continuous, employing legitimate or illegitimate methods, intended in influencing the choice of public affairs and politics, the administration of public works or the choice of political leaders"[9]. Political participation is not just an arbitrary choice but is performed with certain degree of political consciousness and possesses objectives, ideology, programmes, leadership and organisation as important cardinal factors which are interdependent and inter-influential. Political participation of a community is guided by objectives, ideology, programmes, leadership and organisation and incorporates both institutionalised and non-institutionalised individual and collective actions initiated and adopted by a community to achieve desired goals.

Political participation is formed through multiple factors: level of political education, articulated political opinion, amount and quantum of suppression, marginalisation of a particular community, urge for radical changes and many more. It is to be noted that the greater amount of political consciousness would increase and enlarge the level of political participation. It would be observed, in the course of this study, that greater amount of articulated political consciousness among the *Dalit* community has increased throughout the country and broadened level and scope of political participation, particularly since the carious call of Dr. Ambedkar. In fact, there exists a proliferation of consciousness which is felt and expressed politically among the *Dalit* community.

Clubbed with political socialisation, political culture and political participation, political consciousness, thus, becomes 'a functional catalyst' providing general participation, orientations, community mobilisation and identity building processes. As 'a functional catalyst', political consciousness performs tasks of:

1. Subjective understanding of the self;
2. Transmission of knowledge from one generation to another;
3. Objective cognition of socio-eco-politico-cultural conditions;
4. Critical relationship with other communities and structures of powers and economic controls; and
5. Transforming the society consciously with a visionary movement.

Accordingly, political consciousness among the *Dalit* community has shaped a new self-image among them which resolves "will to act against exploitation, rise from oppression, from death to life, from darkness to light"[10] and a tireless zeal to continue their movement for social change and for the establishment of an egalitarian society. The prominent personalities of this movement like Jotiba Phule, Babasaheb Ambedkar and E.V. Ramasami 'Periyar' and others (Narayanaswami Guru in Kerala, Acchutanand in Uttar Pradesh, Mangoo Ram in Punjab) attacked the exploitative system at all and every level: culturally, economically and politically.

There has been an upsurge of the *Dalits* all over India roughly from the *Bhakti* movement (12th to 18th Centuries), which attempted to purify Hinduism of its evils and fought against the tyranny of the caste system. It produced great saints like Chokhamela, Eknath, Pandita Ramabai, Kabir, Ravidas and many more who left an immense appeal, either through their works, preaching or teachings. Later on, Mahatama Jotiba Phule emphasised on educational, social and political development of the community that was, subsequently, articulated by Dr. B.R. Ambedkar who "played three roles: that of a caste leader, that of an untouchable spokesman and that of a national statesman"[11]. He formed three political parties (Independent Labour Party, Scheduled Castes Federation and Republican Party of India) preparing the ground for the *Dalit* Panthers and other formations of the community which are performing task of proliferation of the political consciousness at various levels from understanding of the self to the transformation of society with a visionary movement.

Thus, political consciousness among the *Dalits* incorporates political socialisation, culture and participation in its horizon and possesses value of 'a functional catalyst.' In fact, during the process of exploring the nature of political consciousness among the *Dalits*, one finds that it has a reformatory nature that becomes manifested in the above listed tasks of political consciousness.

Literary Expression

The second definitional perspective includes definition of literature, literary expression and relationship between political consciousness and literary expression.

Literature is not a static collection of written expression authored by a writer nor it is a documentation. Rather it is always evolving and developing keeping tune with the changing times. Literature and its concepts are deeply associated with the development and progress of the society. It is basically the development of the heart of the people and is a cherished asset and accumulation of the knowledge of a particular time period reflecting society in a miroristic way. Literature becomes a christened reflection of the feelings of the masses along with social relation combining it with the literary imagination of a writer[12]. Literature is essentially expression of the reality of human life and great pieces of literature depicts that reality with communicable lucid language facilitating narrative with readers' aesthetic and literary sense having long lasting influence on the heart and mind of the readers. Premchand defines literature as "the critique of life"[13] having spirit of independence, essence of aesthetics, creative soul leading towards the enlightenment of life whether expressed in essay, stories, poetry, novels and autobiographical forms. Literature explores, analyses, understands, investigates and examines several issues of our life and provides' the critique.

Literature is the reflection of a particular time narrating feelings and ideas that are thriving in the heart of the people. It is not just any expression but generates aesthetic sense, movements and strength;

provides mental and spiritual solace; strengthens our determination to overcome difficulties; associates us with the larger social communities and motivates for cherished principles of liberty, equality and solidarity. In this way, literature is not any writing or all the books but as Raymond Williams writes that "Literature is a difficult word, in part because its conventional contemporary meaning appears, at first sight, so simple. There is no apparent difficulty in phrases like English Literature or Contemporary Literature, until we find occasion to ask whether all books and writings constitute literature (and if they are not, which kinds are excluded and by what criteria) or until we make a precise and acceptable distinction between various forms of writings and even oral tradition that is descended through ages"[14].

Literature always explores harmony between Nature and humankind that produces aesthetics, convergence of feelings (between man to man and between authors and readers) and reaffirms mutual love, affection, and ideas of humanity. Literature is not understood as a form of art expressed in a very sophisticated language. Language is just a means to achieve some purpose and it should be easy, communicable and lucid. In fact, great works of literature are those that were written in the language which people speak.[15]

Literature is the imaginative and creative expression of those experiences and events, which are witnessed by the people including the author. The inspiration behind all kinds of literature consists of experiences, feelings, thoughts and ideas drawn from the real life and when blended with creative skills of the authors takes shape of a masterpiece. Any piece of written expression does not become a part of literature unless it generates interest in the socio-politico-cultural milieu, satiate us psychologically and spiritually, make us realise about the real life aesthetic sense, motivates us to overcome, through struggles and movements, our difficulties of life and determines us to consistently make efforts for an egalitarian society for the betterment of humankind and its quality of life ensuring dignity, equality, liberty and solidarity for all.

Literature makes search for harmony and compatibility (between Nature and human being, man to man) its major objectives where love, compassion, mutual self-respect, motion, development, synthesis and fusion of ideas and movements become its cardinal variants for a powerful sense of aesthetics. In fact, literature makes our life more natural and independent which shapes a noble human being.[16]

Like any other branch of human enquiry and intelligence (*e.g.* social sciences and humanities) literature also explores to understand human nature and its numerous manifestations. Here comes a deep relationship between literature and society where any work of literature cannot be devoid or ignorant of the contemporary social reality, of course, it might transcend and represent an idealist view of the social reality that may not, apparently be in consonance with the contemporary social sphere. This relationship is emotional and ever evolving. Going deeper in this relationship would prove that literature is a developmental expression in creative forms that makes us aware, conscious and determined to aspire and achieve our shared vision for a democratic society.

This brings to our notice that the Hindi *Dalit* Literature represents real picture of the community, its trauma and its struggle for social change. This also recognises the fact that literary aesthetics has been transcended from a sophisticated perspective to a realistic aesthetic sense that attempts to demolish the supremacy of structured forms of literary aesthetics. We would explore and analyse this characteristic in subsequent chapters of this study in relation to the Hindi *Dalit* Literature. We would also observe that Hindi *Dalit* Literature is cultivating it own literary space with a very high level of thinking that possesses sense of freedom, essence of realistic aesthetics highlighting ground realities of the *Dalit* community.

In this process, the task, of course, is not to restrict individual creativity but to enhance the greatest possible opportunities of untrammelled development for the individual's creativity blended with the shared common vision of literature. "What can then be seen as happening, in each transition," writes Raymond Williams in 'Marxism and Literature', "is a historical development of social language itself: finding new means, new forms and then new definition of a changing practical consciousness. Many of the active values of 'literature' have then to be seen, not as tied to the concept, which came to limit as well as to summarize them, but as elements of a continuing and changing practice which already substantially, and now at the level of theoretical re-definition, is moving beyond its old forms."[17]

Thus, literature is often considered as mirror, in which society may see its own reflection and it, of course, transcends contemporaneity but many a times represents its own age. It is a record of the torments, hopes and yearnings of a particular age. It gives expression to the aspirations, dreams and vision of the people. When it goes deeper and deeper, it expresses something in the human heart that responds to tears and sorrows more spontaneously than merely to joy and laughter. As a matter of fact, literature aims at true and real depiction of the society where society, in the words of Caudwell, "is like an oyster and literature is its pearl within it".[18] Society is the soil from which the flower of literature springs and makes/motivates this world to be more beautiful and qualitative.

Here it is pertinent to discuss the issue of sociology of literature where there are various schools, *viz.*, Idealist, Positivist, Formalist and Structuralist. Each school of thought has a particular opinion about literature and its relationship with society. We would now elaborate on some of the schools that advocate the sociology of literature and its close interrelation with society and argue vociferously that literature cannot be devoid of its social context, realties and its several connotations.

Idealism

Idealists consider that literature possesses an autonomous sphere and has no or little relation with society. That literature pursues it own aims and attempts to achieve those roles through individual creativity and aesthetic sense. Major proponents of this school are Plato, Aristotle, Hegel and Beneditto Croce.

Plato (427-348 BC) considered that Meta Narrative Consciousness (Idea) is the essence of the universe and external reality is reflection (Form) of that consciousness. His Theory of Idea was philosophically speculated on the premise that this world is in the state of constant flux, in a perpetual flow of ever-changing appearances. He sought to find the permanent in ever changing and called as 'Idea'. "An Idea is not part of the world of time and space. It is eternal; it is the final and independent reality. Idea is an end as well as a source. The world of Ideas is the real world and the familiar world is a world of shadows."[19] All artists and litterateurs attempt to achieve the Idea of Beauty that is independent, imminent and eternal. Idea of Beauty is the source of all creativity and is the Prototype of all Archetypes which thrives to accomplish final Idea of Good, which, in turn, is the source of all Knowledge and Existence. Philosophising the Idea of Good, Plato suggested "both a scientific method of studying complex and involved phenomena and a doctrine involving assertion about degrees of reality. In the former sense, the theory resembles the ideal typology of such modern social scientist as Max Weber, who sought to enlarge our understanding of historical and political reality by imagining institutions and situations relieved of their actual mixture with opposing or contrary tendencies. As a doctrine of reality, the Theory of Idea has both metaphysical and ethical implication. It maintains that the Idea is permanent, consists of objective facts and is not merely convenient human construct. In ethical terms, the Ideas are the implicit goals of their imperfect historical representations and therefore establish a standard by which to judge the world of flux."[20]

Accordingly, literature aims at achieving the Idea of Good and always seeks Prototype of all Archetypes. It is independent and eternal, but Plato qualified this theory when he was constructing his Ideal State that is organic in nature and connects each and every aspect of human activity with each other and represents a fine synthesis of creative artistry and philosophical speculations. In fact, Aristotle (384-322 B.C.), who was not an idealist like Plato but a teleologist, refined this theory and introduced several modifications. He considered that Matter is the Potentiality and the Form is the Actuality and needs an Efficient Cause to become the Final Cause. Aristotle regarded that man becomes 'the efficient cause' imitating nature through art and can discern many alternative potential forms in matter, depending upon the end for which the artistic production is to be used. But even in that the 'final cause' would occur in consonance with the inherent qualities present in matter. Thus, artist has a very crucial role and in a way becomes 'catalyst' to produce the real nature of any phenomena. As Sibley observed that "all this implies that to understand a thing in the ethical, social, and political domain means to know it not merely in its origins and in its history, not only in its parts, as it were, but to know it also in its implicit purpose and its goal...knowledge, therefore, implies an understanding of how every object of knowledge relates to the ordering of the whole; for its function connects its own activities with the purpose or *telos* of the whole"[21]

Expanding the Theory of Knowledge (and Aesthetics), Immanuel Kant (1724-1804), who introduced a new trend which begun with the Rationalism (stressing Reason) of Rene Descartes and the Empiricism (stressing Experience) of Francis Bacon in the philosophical knowledge. Knowledge is an association of ideas or psychological expediency. Philosophy of knowledge consists of two components, *viz.*, rational and sense perception. Knowledge is limited to phenomenon; it cannot know reality as it is. There is a difference between things as they appear and as they are in reality. Appearance is different from reality because in viewing thing, the human mind imposes some qualities on these things, which they do not really possess. But man has pure practical reason that enables him to discover things that are universally valid and binding on him. This discovery enables man to realise that he ought to do certain things. It is this faculty, which takes man beyond the world of phenomenon and leads him to the realisation of the world of reality. Thus, a human being has two aspects of his nature. There is his empirical self, centred on sensual experiences, his desire and impulses. There is also his transcendental self, which is his rational self and which makes him to do what he ought to do. His empirical self, based on desires and impulses, makes him subject to things extraneous to his true self *i.e.*, heteronomous. It is his transcendental self which renders him subject to his true self *i.e.*, autonomous and makes him part of the noumenal, *i.e.*, real world. The final realization of self comes when an individual finds social character of his self, though through transcendental reason and volunteers for the social good. An artist, in fact, depicts any phenomenon with his sensual perception and attempts to transcend it to achieve the noumenal world or the world of reality. Of course, literature, in this way, has linkages with the social phenomena but the realisation of self comes through the 'inward turn' and through the transcendental self of the artist.

G.W.F. Hegel (1770-1831) proclaimed, "reason is the sovereign of the world"[22], truth is the whole, which is merely the essential nature reaching its completeness through the process of its own development of the Absolute. His theory is based on three postulates: that reality is an organic process; all organic processes are dialectical and reality lies in the Ideal and it may be achieved through the realization of *Geist* or Spirit. This Spirit may be called Idea or Reason. It is its nature to realise itself and to reach perfection and history of the world is an attempt on the part of the Spirit or Reason to realise itself though experimentation. The Spirit evolves to higher and higher stages of evolution and self-realisation thought a dialectic process. Thus, the artistic creativity may be achieved through experimentations that undergo a dialectic process to explore the higher and higher stages of self-realisation. Here also, we find that artist is not devoid of the social phenomena but his self-realisation is through a dialectical process with a purpose to achieve the stage of *Geist*.

Italian aesthetician Beneditto Croce[23] (1886-1952) attempted to make all forms of art completely autonomous and considered those forms of art, which are associated with politics as quasi-art. In fact, he was first an aesthetician and then a philosopher and tried to prove that art possesses an autonomous existence. He also contested the viewpoint that advocates philosophising art and aesthetics where, he emphasised that philosophy is based on analytical critique and reason whereas art demands none of these. Art is a very simple, lucid and natural expression that possesses autonomous domain even to the external world. He considers Spirit as Truth that consists of four fundamental processes where two are theoretical, other two are behavioural, and these processes make all forms of art autonomous, authentic and eternal.

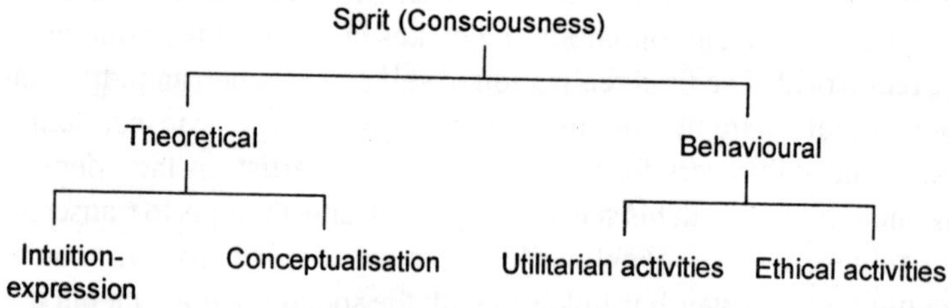

The first of the theoretical processes is intuition-expression where Truth can be experienced through intuitive process. In fact, all kinds of experiences are the instances of consciousness and every human being possesses these instances and a minimal degree of consciousness but there may be differences in terms of degree. Second is the conceptualisation, which is more analytical, rational, and scientific that provides objectivity to comprehend and understand any phenomenon. The practical perspective includes the utilitarian and ethical processes.

All the four processes are different and independent in their nature and scope. Intuition-expression is associated with aesthetics; conceptualisation with logic; utilitarian with economics and ethical is associated with moral. Croce considered the first process (intuition-expression) as the most important, which is also a determined factor for art, literature and aesthetics. It incorporates sensitivity blended with imagination and metaphors that led to the activation of the intuitive-expression producing art, literature and aesthetics. In this way, literature and art are independent of any social factor and has its autonomous domain of operation. But this perspective has its limitation and does not address some of the pertinent issues, in particular that any artist is, after all, located in a socio-cultural milieu and gets affected by its traits. His universe of creation and activities influences his cognition and intuitive-expression.

Positivism

Positivists consider literature as a collective expression of society and attempt to understand it with the cause and effect relationship. Though, it is largely based on the empiricist understanding but it also tries to incorporate various other important components that are important to the understanding the sociology of literature. As Raymond Williams pointed out that "it is now virtually impossible to disentangle a popular sense of positivist from general arguments about Empiricism and scientific method, though the actual history of the word should make us wary of some of its vaguer uses. The word was effectively introduced into French by Comte from 1830 it onwards was often used in English. Its root was positive in one of its developing sense, denoting real or actual existence (a shift from the earliest use to denote 'formally laid down'... the sense of 'definite' or 'certain', in this formal context, obviously contributed to the sense of 'real'). Comte argued that the human mind passed from a primary stage of theological interpretation through a stage of metaphysical and abstract interpretation to a mature stage of positive or scientific understanding, based only on observable facts and the relations between them and the laws discoverable from observing them, all other kinds of inquiry into origin, cause or purpose being pre-scientific. In this sense, positivist was widely adopted and was often interchangeable with scientific… indeed, because it was so concerned with understanding and changing society, it was met by the charge that it was not scientific enough, or not objective enough."[24]

In literature also, it was used as interchangeable with empiricism and as an important instrument to understand society and its reflection in the works of literature. Major proponent of this school was Hippolyte Adolph Taine who, sometimes, is referred as the founder of the discourse that is known as the 'sociology of literature.'

Taine (1828-93), a philosopher, historian and critic of literature and society, made an effort to understand and analyse society and literature and their interrelationships. Taine was writing during the period when Europe was undergoing tremendous social and cultural changes along with Industrial and Scientific revolutions. There was a theoretical change undergoing in the field of social sciences with the beginning of interdisciplinary discourse, influenced by natural sciences and its methods. This was an age where historicity, objectivity and scientificity were being explored to have some convergence.

Elaborating about his literary perspective, Taine regarded that it amounts to be comprehensive and analytical where all aspects of human creativity are facts and events with no value judgements. Scientific analysis means neither appreciating nor condemning any particular thing but analysing it in its totality. Therefore, Taine has a very comprehensive perspective on the works of literature that analyses social facts and events, their processes of production, exploring cause and effect and making it objective. He considered that the purpose of art, literature, science, culture and society is to enrich the repository of knowledge of humankind and the task before a social and cultural scientist is to analyse these facts in a very critical and comprehensive ways so as to represent the true nature of these facts that are affecting the very development of humankind.[25]

There are four major aspects[26] of Taine's sociology of literature, *viz.*,

1. To explore social and material basis of literature;
2. To analyse importance of the author;

3. To interpret reflection of society in the works of literature; and
4. To understand author-reader relation.

In this way, Taine considered literature as the collective expression of society and sociology of literature was established as a discourse that explores, analyses, interprets and understands interrelation between society and literature. In addition to the four major aspects of literature there are three important concepts[27] in Taine's perspective on literature and society:

(*a*) Race as an innate and involving hereditary characteristic;
(*b*) Movement as the epoch, the spirit of the time and as a literary tradition;
(c) Milieu as the environment, emphasising on climate and geography.

These are interconnected concepts and cause the development of literature. Critics of literature have to take into account both the four aspects and three concepts into their consideration so as to achieve a complete and total understanding of any work of literature that is basically derived from the social facts and events thus, in turn, analysing the society at large.

Formalism

In traditional philosophical and aesthetic discourse form denotes the relationship between different elements within a specific system. The term Formalism covered a number of schools in the first half of the twentieth century whose main goal lay in the explanation of the formal and structural patterns of literary texts[28]. This emphasis distinguished itself from older traditions, particularly biographical literary criticism of the nineteenth century, which was primarily concerned with extrinsic or extra-textual features in their analysis of literature. The successive branches of Formalism, the Prague School of Structuralism, New Criticism and Post-structuralism have a common denominator in their general attempts to explain levels of content in relation to formal and structural dimension of texts.

Aristotle introduced the basic philosophical principle, which distinguishes between a level of structure and a level of content into literary criticism, for example in his Poetics (4th century BC) he used the notion of determining function of form over matter for literary phenomena by adopting formal patterns to interpret generic features of drama. This laid down the foundation for subsequent formalist analysis where an attempt was made to know 'how' of the text rather than 'what' of the text.

Russian Formalism started an objective discourse of literary criticism through structural analysis as Roman Jacobson put it "the subject of literary scholarship is not literature in its totality, but literariness, *i.e.*, that which makes of a given work a work of literature."[29] Russian Formalism negates arguments based on spirit, intuition, imagination or genius the of author and neglects historical, sociological, biographical or psychological dimensions of literary discourse. It considered literary work as an independent entity and made phonetic structures, rhythm, rhyme, meter and sound as independent meaningful elements of literary discourse.

According to Victor Shklovski (1893-1984), structural elements in a literary text cause the effect called defamiliarization (stylistic device used to make the reader aware of literary conventions). This tendency, inherent in literary language, counteracts reader's familiarity with everyday language and consequently offers a tool to distinguish between literary and non-literary discourse. He measured novels and poetry from the same yardstick, strongly advocated that literary discourse has nothing to do with social changes, and has an independent existence.

Formalism also tries to structurally, analyse, elements of a text, such as characters in a plot, which earlier schools considered on a thematic level. Vladimir Propp's (1896-1970) character typology, which reduces the indefinite number of characters in literary texts to a limited list of recurrent types, became one of the most important discourses of the Russian Formalism that sustained to till general structural theories of the twentieth century. This kind of analysis and procedure, known as Myth Criticism's, narrowed down the infinite number of possible literary character to a finite number of basic structural agents. Myth Criticism attempts to exposes patterns of myth and the most notable work in this field is that of J.G. Frazer (1854-1941) in this famous work 'Golden Bough' where an effort has been made to unravel the common structures of myth in different historical periods and geographical area. Northrop Frye (1912-91) offered another important approach that placed structure of myth at the heart of what he considered the main literary genres. He resembled patterns of the seasons with that of the literary texts.[30]

Formalist school considers that literature is the product of its own independent existence and has no resemblance with the socio-political discourse. Formalists are of the opinion that literary changes take place due to the 'oldness' in the form of the texts and replace it with another 'new' forms. This change is more geographic rather than socio-political. This school limits vision of the literature and its scope and restricts work to the form of the texts only. This is a very limited way of understanding literature and its relationship with society because it cannot be denied that whatever may be the form, the very content of the literary work cannot be devoid of its social contexts.

Structuralism

A very significant presence was felt by Structuralism in the field of sociology of literature during the mid twentieth century and its major protagonist was Lucien Goldmann (1913-71). He was writing at a time when several streams of literature, philosophy, politics and aesthetics markedly addressed debates on interplay between literature and society. His major contributions include Hidden God (1956), 'Towards a Sociology of the Novel' (1964), 'Cultural Creation in Modern Society' (1976) and 'Methods in the Sociology of Literature' (1980) along with various essays and interviews. He attempted to explore literature with a historical, social and aesthetics perspective making it an analytical instrument for the study of society.

Goldmann considers that literary works are not, in the first place, to be seen as the creation of individuals, but of what he terms, "the Trans individual mental structures"[31] of a social group which are structure of ideas, values, aspiration, thought process and vision. To have a deeper understanding of the literary texts, one should examine structure of thought or 'world vision' of the social class or group to which the writer belongs. "Great writers are those exceptional individuals who manage to transpose into the world vision of the class or group to which they belong, and to do this in a peculiarly unified and translucent way."[32] He termed his critical method 'genetic structuralism'[33] which helped to understand, interpret and analyse literary works.

Explaining the unique character of this method Terry Eagleton writes that it is important to understand both terms of genetic structuralism. "Structuralism, because Goldmann is less interested in the contents of a particular world vision than the structure of categories it displays. Two apparently quite different writers may thus be shown to belong to the same collective mental structure. Genetic, because Goldmann is concerned with how such mental structures are historically produced-concerned, that is to say, with the relations between a world vision and the historical conditions which give rise to it"[34]. Eagleton further elucidates, "what Goldmann is seeking, then, is a set of structural relations between literary text, world vision and history itself. He wants to show how the historical situation of a social groups or class is transposed, by the mediation of its world vision into the structure of a literary work. To do this it is not enough to begin with the text and work outwards to history or vice versa; what is required is a dialectical method of criticism which moves constantly between text, world vision and history, adjusting each to the others."[35]

Introducing Method in the Sociology of Literature, William Q. Boelhower writes that "in order to conceptualise the levels of the cultural creation of society, the '*sine qua non*' of a valid sociological aesthetics, Goldmann collected certain macro-analytical categories (totality, world view, form, the transinidividual subject and possible consciousness-objective possibility) from Lukacs and grounded them in a series of positive and anthropological categories taken from Piaget (significant structure, function, the structuration-destructuration process, the epistemological circle of the subject and object, equilibrium). His intention was to convert the categories the Lukacs used in a philosophical and merely descriptive way into methodological prototypes that would prove to be highly functional, rather that ideological instruments."[36] Thus literary works, for Goldmann should be seen as structure and not devoid of its context (socio-politico-historical). If a text is not analysed with this perspective then the very 'sociality' of the text and its communicability could not be captured that may lead to flawed understanding of the contexts of its generation. Hence, socio-aesthetic unity of the text is very crucial to understand and analyse the society. It is of utmost importance because the very generation of literary works can never be devoid of its context and no writer can ever be so autonomous and independent of his/her milieu. The method developed by Goldmann (genetic structuralism) considers literary works a constitutive element of social consciousness that shape the very structure of any text. He provided six analytical tools that make his method a comprehensive one and include Significant Structure, Trans individual Subject, Totality, World View, Possible Consciousness-objective possibility and Homology, thus making the field of sociology of literature a challenging one that not only analyses a particular text but the overall contexts, its several connotations and its processes that lad to the creation of a text. This again reaffirms the fact that there exists a very intrinsic interrelation between politics and literature.

Sociological Literary Criticism

Sociological literary criticism also considers a close interrelation between creative literature and politics and emphasises on the contexts of the text. Before discussing major protagonist of this school, it is important to understand the meaning of the term criticism and literary criticism. "Criticism has become a very difficult word", writes Raymond Williams "because its predominant general sense is of fault-finding has an underlying sense of judgement and a very confusing specialised sense, in relation to art and literature."[37] History of the term 'criticism' has travelled a long journey from 'negative judgement' to 'the distinction of appreciation' and now takes into account various concepts such as judgement, discrimination, sensibility, disinterested, qualified, rigorous and so on in its orbit expanding its horizon. Literary criticism can refer to systematic and scholarly interpretation of texts as well as their evaluation.

Sociological Literary Criticism makes an attempt to interpret literary texts on the basis of their contexts, connotations, interpretation and evaluation. It starts with the assumption that any creative work cannot be produced in a vacuum and has deep connection with the socio-political context. Leo Lowenthal has made remarkable contribution in this field though Adorno and Marcuse have also attempted to develop sociology of aesthetics and literature. All of them were writing during the interwar period under the aegis of the Frankfurt School that explored Critical Theory. There are three important contributory works by Leo Lowenthal *viz.*, Literature and the Image of Man, Literature, Popular Culture and Society and The Art of the Narrative and Society. Considering himself as 'literary scientist', Lowenthal regarded that the aim of literature lies in the analysis of its sociality. He started with an understanding that literature has the power to tap aesthetic sensibilities of the society and its time. Literature is the expression of socio-politico-historical experiences and provides insights about the contemporary human life. Social reality can be reflected in literature only when the author is conscious of his/her social aesthetic sensibilities, hence, it is important to understand the author's perspective to analyse creative works. This characteristic makes author as the 'ideologue' of his time and according to Lowenthal, author cannot remain 'just neutral' to the contemporary social reality.

According to Lowenthal, there are two kinds of consciousness in the expression of literature *i.e.*, singular consciousness and plural consciousness where the former is expressed throughout a particular text and makes itself 'ideological' while the latter is expressed through a dialectical process of consciousness and makes it more complex but realistic as the social reality itself is a complex process to understand and analyse. He utilised dialectical materialism as an important instrument for sociological literary criticism. For him, both form and content are important constituents of creative literature where content can be analysed with the sociological methods (for Lowenthal, it was dialectical materialism) and form may be analysed with the aesthetic method (here he tries to combine Adorno and Marcuse). A fine blending of form and content reflecting the social reality would have an impact on the reader that would also provide him/her insights to comprehend, understand and analyse the contemporary social reality and his/her connectivity with the structures of society. In this way, Lowenthal made important contribution in the field of sociology of literature making it a scientific analytical tool for the interpretation of social reality, capturing nuances of the complexities of social structures and levels of consciousness.

His works established the fact that literature and socio-political context cannot be isolated.

Marxist School

For the study of the literary expression of political consciousness Marxism is the most notable school that attempts to deliver both a 'Theory' and 'Method' for literary criticism. Though there are difficulties in arriving at a monolithic Marxist literary theory, as Terry Eagleton puts it that "Marx and Engels had rather more important tasks on their hands than the formulation of a complete aesthetic theory. Their comments on art and literature are scattered and fragmentary, glancing allusions rather than developed positions. This is one reason why Marxist criticism involves more than merely re-stating cases set out by the founders of Marxism. It also involves more than what has become known in the West as the 'sociology of literature'. The sociology of literature concerns itself chiefly with what might be called the means of literary production, distribution and exchange in a particular society-how books are published, the social composition of their authors and audiences, levels of literacy, the social determinants of 'taste'. It also examines literary texts for their 'sociological relevance, raiding literary works to abstract from themes of interest to the social historian."[38] He further elaborates, "Marxist criticism is not merely a sociology of literature, concerned with how novels get published and whether they mention the working class. Its aim is to explain the literary work more fully; and this means a sensitive attention to its forms, styles and meanings. But it also means grasping those forms, styles and meanings as the products of a particular history... The originality of Marxist criticism, then, lies not in its historical approach to literature but in its revolutionary understanding of history itself."[39]

Marxist criticism is based on the assumption that literature is the product of its historical context and cannot be isolated from its contemporary context. As Marx and Engels wrote in 'The German Ideology, that "the production of ideas, concepts and consciousness is first of all directly interwoven with the material intercourse of man, the language of real life. Conceiving, thinking, the spiritual intercourse of men, appear here as the direct efflux of men's material behaviour... we do not proceed from what men say, imagine, conceive, nor from men as described, thought of, imagined, conceived, in order to arrive at corporeal man; rather we proceed from the really active man...consciousness does not determine life: life determines consciousness."[40] They further wrote in the Preface of A Contribution to the Critique of Political Economy "the mode of production of material life conditions the social, political and intellectual life process in general. It is not the consciousness of men that determines their being, but on the contrary, their social being that determines their consciousness."[41] Thus art and artistic creation become constituent of the 'superstructure' and its 'base' is provided by the economic mode of production but Marxist criticism is very cautious about the mechanical and one-to-one correspondence between base and superstructure.

Literature, for this school, is, of course, a part of the superstructure but it is not just the passive reflection of the economic base though it considers that art cannot change the course of history but it can be an active element in such changes. Marx clearly pointed out that there exists 'the unequal relationship of the development of material production...to the artistic production' as he says that "in the case of the arts, it is well know that certain periods of their flowering are out of all proportion to the general development of society, hence also to the material foundation, the skeletal structure, as it were, of its organisation...it is even recognised that certain forms of art, *e.g.* the epic, can no longer be produced in their world epoch-making, classical stature as soon as the production of art, as such begins; that is, that certain significant forms within the realm of the arts are possible only at an undeveloped stage of artistic development. If this is the case with the relation between different kinds of art within the realm of art, it is already less puzzling that it is the case in the relation of the entire realm to the general development of society. The difficulty consists only in the general formulation of these contradictions. As soon as they have been specified, they are already clarified."[42] This kind of difficulty leads us to examine works of literature from a very comprehensive perspective so as to arrive at a meaningful understanding of the contemporary social reality and its expression in the creative literature.

It also associates works of literature that represents certain ideological viewpoints signifying the ways men live out their class roles in society, the values, ideas and images which tie them to their social functions. At the same time literature challenges the ideological viewpoints also as Ernst Fischer advocates that "authentic art always transcends the ideological limits of its time, yielding us insight into the realities which ideology hides from the view."[43] French Marxist theorist Louis Althusser also regards that literature remains unrestricted by ideology but it has a very 'particular relationship with it'.[44]

Another important component of Marxist literary criticism is that of the form and content though many critics have discussed it in limited ways. In fact, form has been considered 'stylistic exercise' and it has to represent content of the social reality. Marx himself regarded that "mere stylistic exercise led to 'perverted content', which in turn impresses the stamp of 'vulgarity' on literary form. He shows a dialectical grasp of the relations in question: form is the product of content, but reacts back upon it in a double-edged relationship. Marx's early comment about oppressively formalistic law in the *Rheinische Zeitung* – 'form is now of value unless it is the form of its content'- could equally be applied to his aesthetic views".[45] Therefore, form and content are dialectically related and "form is produced by content, is identical and one with it, and, though the primacy is on the side of content, form reacts on contents and never remains passive".[46] Christopher Caudwell also reaffirms that content determines the expression of form and it is only content that brings change in the form and its various mode of expression. According the Terry Eagleton "form is always a complex unity of at least three elements: it is partly shaped by a 'relatively autonomous' literary history of forms; it crystallizes out of certain dominant ideological structures and it embodies a specific set of relations between author and audience. It is the dialectical unity between these elements that Marxist criticism is concerned to analyse."[47]

Thus Marxist literary criticism is based on the theory of 'base' and 'superstructure' analysing literature with the method of dialectical materialism representing the ideological viewpoints of the author and his times and attempts a unity between form and content. We would discuss two major protagonists of this school, Georg Lukacs and Raymond Williams.

Georg Lukacs (1885-1971) represented a period of intellectual critique and political turmoil. He was writing at a time when most of the European intellectual discourse was passing through a process of reconstruction. He was a philosopher, aesthetician and political activist and to understand his contribution one has to go deeper to the times of his writings. He regarded that the literature should be representative of its times and the great writers are those who can capture and recreate a harmonious totality of human life. His major works include Studies in 'The Historical Novel' (1962), 'The Meaning of Contemporary Realism' (1969), 'European Realism' (1972), 'Aesthetics' (1962) and 'History and Class Consciousness' (1923).

Lukacs understanding of society and literature is guided by an attempt to capture many-sided image of human wholeness. Terry Eagleton describes that Lukacs has a very clear understanding of society and of the 'writers' "where the general and the particular, the conceptual and the sensuous, the social and the individual are increasingly torn apart by the 'alienation' of capitalism, the great writer draws them dialectically together into a complex totality" representing Lukacs' "fiction in a microcosmic form, the complex totality of society itself."[48] He called such an endeavour 'Realism' and considered ancient Greece, the Renaissance period and France in the early nineteenth century as the three great periods of historical realism. "A realist work is rich in a complex, comprehensive set of relations between man, nature and history."[49]

Totality, typicality, reflection and historical world are the major critical concepts in the works of Lukacs and they possess an interrelated existence to express the true nature of social reality. "A typical or representative character incarnates historical forces without thereby ceasing to be richly individualised; and for a writer to dramatize those historical forces he must, for Lukacs, be progressive in his art"[50]. Reflection means objectivity of art and artist, which is not mechanical, passive and photographic. Only objective comprehension of the historical forces are able to express complex level of consciousness and it is a challenging task before the artist to express these forces with objective form. Internal dynamics of these critical concepts make any particular work of literature transcendental and provides insights to understand the contemporary historical process. For Lukacs, great artist are those who create great piece of works, not due to their personal stylistic skills but due to their objective comprehension of the historical forces and locates his/her position within history. It is important to recall that this kind of understanding leads us to reiterate that there exists a very intrinsic relationship between creative literature and politics and it is more important in the context of Hindi *Dalit* Literature as it is the product of such historical forces which are shaping future of *Dalit* community and movement in the contemporary Indian society.

Another important contribution in the Marxist literary criticism has been made by Raymond Williams (1921-88) who was a man of varieties. His writings include 'Culture and Society' (1958), The 'Long Revolution' (1961), 'Modern Tragedy' (1966), 'Orwell' (1971), 'The Country and the City' (1973), 'Keywords' (1976) and 'Marxism and Literature' (1977). Some critics regard that there are three stages in the development of thought of Raymond Williams; the first stage starts with his works like 'Reading and Criticism' (1950) and 'Drama: From Ibsen to Eliot' (1952) with gradually moving towards Marxism; the second stage is represented in the works like 'Culture and Society' and 'The Long Revolution' and the third one is expressed in the works like 'The Country and the City' and 'Marxism and Literature.' During all these stages he was attempting to explore a theory of culture, literature and society continuing his debates with three major discourses, *viz.*, Romanticism, Rational Criticism and Marxism and analysing Wordsworth, Arnold, Eliot, Lewis, Marx, Engels, Caudwell, Goldmann and Lukacs. This sort of analyses makes him a quintessential philosopher, theoretician, sociologist, political thinker, and a sensitive litterateur.

Investigating critically the origin of the term literature and its different usages, Raymond Williams produced a remarkable work 'Marxism and Literature' where he dealt with the subject extensively. He starts with the origin itself and writes "in its modern form the concept of 'literature' did not emerge earlier than the eighteenth century and was not fully developed until the nineteenth century. Yet the conditions for its emergence had been developing since the Renaissance. The word itself came into English use in the fourteenth century following French and Latin precedents: its root was Latin *littera*, a letter of the alphabet. Literature in the common early spelling was then in effect a condition of reading: of being able to read and of having read."[51]

According to his theorisation, literature was not, initially, a work of imagination, reflection of society in its true nature or of production and included philosophy, history and essays and as well as poems. With the advent of print (and print capitalism) literature transformed its nature and scope leading towards 'an objective category' that constitute taste or sensibility as a criterion defining literary quality; an increasing specialization of literature to creative or imaginative works and a development of the concept of tradition within national terms, resulting in the more effective definition of a national literature. Raymond Williams identified the development of literature and its shift from mere reading to the expression of contemporary times from the Renaissance to the days of the Marxism. He clearly established the fact that journey of literature has complex nature and it is important to understand the very nature of its journey to comprehend properly the scope of literature.[52] This view is in resonance with the journey of Hindi *Dalit* Literature which itself has travelled a long way, of course, with the *Dalit* movement and transforming its nature from the 'reformative' and 'moralistic' to 'political' which attempts to reflect the objective cognition of contemporary social structures.

Emphasising the importance of Marxist tradition, Raymond Williams writes that it has "attempted assimilation of 'literature' to 'ideology'...an effective and important inclusion of 'popular literature'—the 'literature of the people'—as a necessary part of the literary tradition, and a sustained but uneven attempt to relate 'literature' to the social and economic history within which 'it' had been produced. Each of these last two attempts has been significant. In the former a 'tradition' has been genuinely extended. In the latter there has been an effective reconstitution, over wide areas, of historical social practice, which makes the abstraction of 'literary values' much more problematical..."[53]

He also identified 'significant tendencies' of Marxist literary criticism where Lukacs contributed a profound revaluation of 'the aesthetic'; the Frankfurt School, with its special emphasis on art, and undertook a sustained re-examination of 'artistic production', centred on the concept of 'mediation' and Goldmann undertook a radical revaluation of the 'creative subject'. Making literature a tool to understand social transition, Raymond William pointed out explicitly that "what can then be seen as happening, in each transition, is a historical development of social language itself; finding new means, new forms and then new definitions of a changing practical consciousness. Many of the active values of literature have then to be seen, not as tied to the concept, which came to limit as well as to summarize them, but as elements of a continuing and changing practice which already substantially, and now at the level of theoretical redefinition, is moving beyond its old forms".[54] Literary theory is defined by its capacity to capture these transitions along with the perception of beauty, 'contemplation of an object and perception and contemplation of the 'making' of an object', its language, its skill of construction and its aesthetic properties. In this way, Raymond Williams provided a comprehensive literary theory that included various 'schools' but has distinction of its own emphasising on 'structure of sensibility' that has to take into its consideration the very processes of artistic creation and its production. Of course, there might be different views on his theorisation but one thing can be said that he attempted to integrate contemporary debates on art and literature with society utilising the instrument of dialectical materialism. In fact, the apparent changes in his positions also represent dilemma of his times and he endeavoured to reflect these dilemmas in a very cohesive manner producing systematic and exhaustive theory of literary criticism.

Thus seen, every school of the sociology of literature (except Idealist) considers that there exists a very close interplay between society, politics and literature. Each school has its positives and its negatives but none of these schools are mutually contradictory and also excel in the understanding of each other where Positivists highlight the importance of social fact to be expressed in the literary text; Formalists emphasise on form and are not devoid of content; Structuralists pointed out the role of structures in the creation of literary texts; Literary Criticism provides insights into the sociality of literary text and Marxists advocate that literature cannot be isolated from its socio-historical contexts. Keeping in mind the close relationship between creative expression and political consciousness, it is pertinent to study grassroots level political movements so as to acquire a comprehensive view of the movements. This is more important for the study of the *Dalit* movement in Hindi belt as this movement is articulating itself in making its political identity and expressing it with all cultural and literary mediums. Thus it is very much relevant for the understanding of the contemporary political movement to study it through the literary expressions.

Analysis of these ideological debates provide comprehensive theoretical framework for this study as the central theme revolves around political consciousness among *Dalits* as expressed in Hindi *Dalit* Literature, which, by its very nature, is a 'protest literature' which has its roots in the contemporary *Dalit* Movement. We find direct bearings of the socio-political context in the expression of Hindi *Dalit* Literature, for instance, when Premchand was writing *Godan*, he was locating it within the contemporary socio-political contexts while there was a National Liberation Movement, struggle against imperialism and colonialism and most notable was the Gandhian outlook that considered problems of the *Dalit* community in the Indian society as moralistic. While the recent writings in the Hindi *Dalit* Literature represent a political outlook and indicates the transition that took place through *Dalit* movement in the contemporary Indian society.

Different schools of sociology of literature also provide an opportunity to make an effort towards the construction of the theory of *Dalit* aesthetics. *Dalit* aesthetics is not merely a concern of literature discussing forms, style and language used for the expression of political consciousness among *Dalits* but needs a thorough understanding of the Indian social structure and locating Hindi *Dalit* Literature in that perspective. Given the context of the *Dalit* community, it is of utmost importance that an attempt should be made to establish a sociological aesthetics of *Dalit* Literature rather than just a literary aesthetics of the literature. Following section would investigate how Hindi *Dalit* Literature is deeply placed in its socio-politico-historical contexts and how political consciousness which is expressed through literature also depicts the true nature of the *Dalit* community in the contemporary social structure.

Placing Hindi *Dalit* Literature

The focus of the present study is to explore nature and scope of literary expression of political consciousness among *Dalits* with the objective to investigate the larger relationship between creative literature and politics. Some of the works of Hindi Literature have been selected to explore this relationship. We have already discussed different schools of thought in the preceding section and now we would discuss how the context of the *Dalit* community and their movements have affected/influenced the very course of literary expression of political consciousness in Hindi Literature. Though history of *Dalit* movement would be discussed in the next chapter, this section is devoted to understand the influence of political trends on the expression of literary works and how this study can be placed in its socio-political contexts with their different connotations.

First of all, it is important to notice that the Hindi *Dalit* Literature, by its very nature is a protest literature as it protests very vociferously against multiple levels the oppression perpetrated on this section of Indian society through the perpetuation of the Indian Caste System and its inherent oppressive nature. The *Dalit* Literature is an integral part of the *Dalit* Movement as it utilizes different forms, styles and content which is inherently political for its expression. It cannot be studieds isolating from its contemporary context, as it is not a 'recreational' or 'leisure' literature because it advocates rights of the *Dalit* community and inspires people to rise against oppression.

Though *Dalit* literature in Marathi is a well-established stream, the Hindi *Dalit* Literature is a product of recent socio-political development at the grassroots levels. Tracing the roots of the *Dalit* literature Eleanor Zelliot writes, "While *Dalit* literature as a school, a self-conscious movement, is a product of the 1960s. Individual writers from among the Untouchables appear in the fourteenth century and again in the Mahar movement, which began in the late nineteenth century. In the long history of Marathi literature before the 1960s, only one school of acknowledged writers included members of the lower castes-that of *Bhakti* saint-poets. Popular entertainment-*lawani* (Ballads), *pawads* (Panegyric poetry) and folk-dramas called *tamasha*, undoubtedly were produced by low castes, but were anonymous and were never considered as respectable literature. The *Bhakti* movement, begun traditionally by Dyaneshwar in the thirteenth century, was joined by saint-poets from almost all Marathi-speaking castes, including the Mahar poet-Chokhamela. Two of the most popular *Bhakti* saints are the *Shimpi* (tailor) Namdeo, a contemporary of Chokhamela in the fourteenth century, and the last and greatest of the saints-poets, the Maratha-Kunbi Tukaram in the seventeenth century. Dyaneshwar himself was an outcaste Brahman and another major figure in the *Bhakti* pantheon, the saint, Eknath, of the sixteenth century, kept his *Brahmanical* standing only by virtue of miracles performed with the help of Vithoba, the God of the *Bhakti* movement."[55]

Zelliot has further traced the very course of the development of Marathi *Dalit* Literature which has a corresponding parallels in the political changes faced by the Marathi society and the *Dalit* community. In this regard Zelliot quotes Vasudha Mane's piece on 'Recent Marathi Writing' that highlighted the context of the *Dalit* Literature "in a society which is still caste-ridden, the new crop of writers belonging to castes and classes which were traditionally outside the pale of literature so far has attracted attention during the past few years in Marathi literature. They come from backward rural areas, from slums in industrial towns and many of them hail from families of labourers and menials. They come with experiences hitherto unknown and unimagined by the most sympathetic and observant of writers in the traditionally literate classes. They come with a language and expression which has trampled all conventions"[56] Further, Zelliot found that "there is, of course, a focus on the life of the lowly in *Dalit* literature" with variations in "the style and content" and "suffering tinged with hope".[57]

There was also a very significant impact of Black American Literature on the *Dalit* Literature and writers found a 'parallel phenomenon' in their movements. "Janardan Waghmare has written extensively of the possible comparison between Black and *Dalit*, pointing out that although the Black was brought to America from Africa, the *Dalit* was born in his own country. He may have been an heir of this country but he could not claim his heritage... so Ambedkar said, "Gandhiji, I have no homeland..."[58] Zelliot further noted that "there is an occasional reference to the Black world in *Dalit* literature, such as in Daya Pawar's poem entitled "Harlem," which is a love poem to his wife with full realization of the life-destroying world around them. There seems, however, to be no imitation of Black literature and its two strongest fields, autobiography and dramas, are not yet developed in *Dalit* literature."[59] But we would notice, in the fourth chapter, that Hindi *Dalit* Literature has initiated process with these two fields also by Mohan Dass Naimishray's '*Apne Apne Pinjare*' and Om Prakash Balmiki's '*Joothan*' expressing their biographical account. But the major contribution of this comparison remains important and found American Black Literature "as support, as proof that a group similar to the *Dalit* can become militant, can become creative, and can progress in a hostile society".[60]

Highlighting the role of cultural movement in the politics of Maharashtra, Gopal Guru in his book *Dalit* Cultural Movement and Dialectics of *Dalit* Politics in Maharashtra writes that *Dalit* cultural movement has performed two historical tasks: one, it has generated different forms of literature of its own community (like poetry, drama, autobiography etc.) paving the way for the realization of the cultural and literary aspirations and two, it has prepared a radical context for the politics and political movements initiated by Dr. B.R. Ambekar.[61] Thus, the *Dalit* literature has a revolutionary vision for social change establishing an egalitarian society and travels its journey with the *Dalit* movement in Indian society. The very agenda of the *Dalit* literature was political and aspires for structural changes in the society in all fields: social, political, cultural and economic. We find a direct influence of political movement on the *Dalit* literature, for example, Maharashtra experienced Ambedkar's influence in the first half of the last century itself who made *Dalit* issue a 'political' rather than the 'moral' one as against Gandhi for whom *Dalit* issue was a 'moral' issue. In the same way, Marathi *Dalit* Literature was also expressing these trends in hundreds of works having a convergence with the Ambedkarite movement.

In contrast to the society in Maharashtra, North Indian society experienced a different kind of response to the *Dalit* issue, and the very tone of the social texture was 'reformative'. In Uttar Pradesh, Swami Acchutananda (1879-1933) launched '*Adi Hindu* Movement' during nineteenth century and anti-caste literature was written that focused on highlighting the multiple oppressions faced by the *Dalit* community. In fact, the roots of *Adi Hinduism* can be traced in the *Bhakti* movement itself that advocated equality but Adi Hindu Ideology constructed a theory of the ancient racial origin of 'untouchables' and claimed original inhabitancy. Shankarnand also wrote, attacking the caste system, vary powerful poetry which became popular in the oral tradition during the nineteenth century and influenced the community sensitising them for 'a changed thinking'.

Dayananda Saraswati also made an attempt to reform the caste system and Arya Samaj "promised to facilitate the social uplift of lower castes, set up schools for them, and presented the hope of surmounting caste division by allowing untouchables to enter the Hindu caste hierarchy through 'purification' or *shuddhi*... but the symbols that the Samaj usually upheld was the Vedas, which were projected as the ultimate container of religious truths. The growing emphasis on the Vedas by the Arya Samaj, however, implied the fortification of caste distinctions on which the Vedas were based. This gradually disillusioned the untouchable who had joined it, especially because the Samaj did not accord them equality of status, even though it admitted lower caste to the Hindu hierarchy through *shuddhi*. The distinction between high-cast Hindus and the 'purified' low castes had remained."[62] We find that there was a very vocal *Adi Hindu* Movement in the Hindi belt during the first half of the last century led by Swami Acchutananda and Baba Ram Charan, its major protagonists, that had a significant impact on course of *Dalit* politics and also its expression in literature.

There was an inspiration from the *Bhakti* movement but its focus was not reformatory rather it introduced introspective dimension of *Bhakti* and gave it a new social significance. "Spiritual introspection (*atma-anubhav*) was accorded supreme importance as the only way to arrive at true knowledge or *sadgyan* and to evolve one's own world view"[63] as Acchutanand said, "Real knowledge is the knowledge gained through introspection and which you have understood and realized on your own. For this reason, you will have to discern between good and evil, virtue and vice, auspicious and inauspicious, through your own introspection. This [introspection] is the path of self-realization of the *sants* [saints and preachers]. Self-realization is the only touchstone against which you can test truth and falsity, high and low."[64] This movement had an impact on the course of the *Dalit* movement in Hindi belt but it got fully articulated with the advent of Ambedkar on contemporary socio-political scene. Though his presence was belated as expressed by Mohan Dass Naimishray who writes, "There were Kabir, Nanak and Raidas in the north but not Jotiba Phule and Ambedkar and this is a matter of regret for this belt because they advocated revolutionary changes in the very structure of this caste-ridden society."[65]

Mohan Dass Naimishray further traced the prevalent Hindi *Dalit* Literature which, in his opinion, "remained ignored or unrecognised by the elite or upper-castes."[66] He writes that Ramchand Banodha from Allahabad wrote a biography much before Dhananjay Keer and there were several authors inspired by Dr. Ambedkar and wrote very powerful *Dalit* literature, for instance, Bhagwandas Yadvendu (Acchut ka Beta), Dr. Khemchand Bohre, Babu Karan Singh Kain, Gopi Chand Pippal and Chatrapati Ambesh. Since there was not a strong *Dalit* movement in this belt, these writings remained either ignored or unrecognised. Here we notice how politics affects the very course of literature in society whereas Maharashtrian society was able to enrich itself with the cultural movement along with the political movement but Hindi society experienced a different kind of literature because there were no visible available references to it.

The decade of 1980s was a watershed mark in the history of the *Dalit* movement in Hindi belt. The contemporary socio-political structures were having new interfaces with the changing patterns of the society and new social forces were unleashing themselves making their claim on the political system. *Dalit* politics shaped its identity by this time and there were various organizations articulating *Dalit* voice. We would examine these trends and patterns in the next chapter but it is to be noted that *Dalit* politics during this decade attempted to incorporate each and every expression of the *Dalit* voice including literature making it a larger and comprehensive movement for social change visualizing equality, liberty and justice in an egalitarian social structure. We would also discuss different views about *Dalit* aesthetics and form and style of the Hindi *Dalit* Literature, which has a very close relation with the form, and style of the *Dalit* politics in the Hindi belt.

Highlighting close relation between political movement and *Dalit* Literature, Dr. Sharan Kumar Limbale pointed out that there were hopes and aspiration at the time of Independence that trauma and pain of the *Dalit* community would come to end but this oppression continued along with many other problems like unemployment, poverty, caste conflicts, casteisation of politics that compounded the miseries of human life and made it complicated. But with the proliferation of democratic values to the depth of Indian social set-up clubbed with the expansion of education started the process of agitation and protest against the oppression and reaffirm the principles of equality, independence, justice and solidarity which led to the revolutionary changes in the vision of the political movement and literary expression reflected these changes in the vision to represent the social reality of the contemporary time.[67] Contemporary Hindi *Dalit* Literature is the result of the impact of Ambedkarite vision for revolutionary change and aesthetics of this literature makes democracy, egalitarian social vision and humane values its essence. The very inspiration behind Hindi *Dalit* Literature is political that gets influenced by the Ambedkar movement, consolidation of democracy in India, proliferation of science and technology, political articulation by the new social forces and universalization of education making it a comprehensive domain for analysis that is representative of the contemporary Indian social and political reality.

Dalit Literature expresses the political consciousness that focused on the struggle for self-respect and dignity and carves a 'new self-image' for the community and it is also self-critical and introspective in its nature and scope, which sometimes play a role of guiding force to the political movement. It also visualizes the trends in the political movements, as would be seen during the course of this study, providing an opportunity for adopting the right course of action during the *Dalit* movement. Hindi *Dalit* Literature represents the *Dalit* voice and community's "movement against socio-economic exploitation and numerous types of atrocities committed on the *Dalits*; movements for better access to the opportunities and for realization of goals of equality, liberty, fraternity and justice; and finally the movements for gaining self-respect and dignified social identity."[68]

It also represents struggle against oppression and sets a positive agenda before itself exploring Independence and Democracy and making each and every person equal having equal rights, liberty and freedom. Representation of political discourse makes Hindi *Dalit* Literature political literature and its expression of political consciousness becomes literary enriching it and enthusing confidence within the community that sustains their movement.

The Hindi *Dalit* Literature is representing real picture of the *Dalit* community, its trauma and its struggle for social change. This also recognises the fact that literary aesthetics have transcended from a *'sophisticated'* perspective to a realistic aesthetic sense that attempts to demolish the 'supremacy of structured forms' (of the upper castes writers) of literary aesthetics. We would explore and analyse this characteristic in subsequent chapters of this study in relation to the Hindi *Dalit* Literature. We would discuss, in the next chapter, the markers of *Dalit* aesthetics and how those markers are political in their nature. Also a brief history of *Dalit* movement would be narrated in next chapter with an attempt to trace different literary trends in the expression of political consciousness of *Dalits*'.

NOTES

1. *Penguin Dictionary of Psychology* (Second edition), New York, Arther S. Reber, 1984.
2. Please see George H. Sabine, *A History of Political Theory* (Third edition) (Delhi: Oxford & IBH Publishing Co., 1961); William Ebenstein, *Great Political Thinkers* (Third edition) (Delhi: Oxford & IBH Publishing Co., 1969); C.L. Wayper, *Political Thought* (Delhi: B.I. Publications, 1974); M.Q. Sibley, *Political Ideas and Ideology: A History of Political Thought* (Delhi: Surjeet Publications, 1981); David Robertson, *The Penguin Dictionary of Politics* (London: Penguin Books, 1985); S.P. Verma, *Modern Political Theory: A Critical Survey* (1989 edition) (Delhi: Vikas Publishing House, 1989) and Goodin & Pettit (ed.), *A Companion to Contemporary Political Philosophy* (Blackwell Publishers, 1993) for further detail.
3. Johari, J.C. *Comparative Politics* (Delhi: Sterling Publishers, 1979) p. 4.
4. Oakeshoot, Michael. *Political Education* (Cambridge, 1952) p. 15.
5. *Ibid.*
6. Tawney, R.H. *Equality* (New York: Harcourt Brace, 1931) p. 230.
7. Dahl, Robert A. *Modern Political Analysis* (Fifth edition) (Delhi: Prentice Hall of India, 1997) p. 12-48.
8. Almond, Gabriel A. & Powell, G.B. Jr. *Comparative Politics: A Developmental Approach* (Boston: Little Brown, 1966) p. 64.
9. Weiner, Myron. *Ibid.*, p. 164.
10. Omvedt, Gail. *Ibid.*, p. 11.
11. Zelliot, Eleanor. *Ibid.*, p. 53.
12. Please see Raymond Williams, *Keywords: A Vocabulary of Culture & Society* (London: Fontana Press: 1983) and *Marxism and Literature* (Oxford: Oxford University Press 1977); Terry Eagleton, *Marxism and Literary Criticism* (London: Methuen & Co. Ltd, 1976); Philip Green & Michael Walzer, *The Political Imagination in Literature* (New York: Free Press, 1969): Marxs & Engels, *On Literature & Art* (Moscow: Progress Publishers, 1978); Sujit Mukherjee, *Towards a Literary History of India* (Simla: Indian Institute of

Advanced Study, 1975); Hazari Prasad Dwivedi, *Hindi Sahitya:Udbhav aur Vikas* (Sixth edition) (Delhi: Rajkamal Prakashan, 1990); Manager Pandey, *Sahitya Ke Samajshastra ki Bhoomika* (Chandigarh: Harayana Sahitya Academy,1989) for further detail.

13. Premchand, *Sahitya Ka Uddeshya* in People's Art in the Twentieth Century: Theory & Practice (Delhi: Jana Natya Manch, July 99-September 2000) p. 75.
14. Williams, Raymond. *Ibid.*, p. 183.
15. Premchand. *Ibid.*, p. 74.
16. *Ibid.*, p. 77.
17. Williams, Raymond. *Marxism and Literature* (Oxford: Oxford University Press, 1977) p. 54.
18. Please see Christopher Caudwell. *Illusion and Reality: A Study of the Sources of Poetry* (Delhi: People's Publishing House, 1991) for further detail.
19. Wayper, C.L. *Ibid.*, p. 18-20.
20. Sibley, Mulford Q. *Ibid.*, p. 64.
21. *Ibid.*, p. 88.
22. Wayper, C.L. *Ibid.*, p. 161-170.
23. Please see Benedetto Croce, *Aesthetic as Science of Expression and General Linguistics*, Translated by Douglas Aindie (1929 edition); *The Defence of Poetry: Variations on the Theme of Shelly*, Translated by E.F. Carrit, 1933; *Aesthetics*, entry in the Encyclopaedia Britannica, Vol. I, p. 263-72, 1953 edition for further detail.
24. Williams, Raymond. *Keywords: A Vocabulary of Culture & Society* (London: Fontana Press, 1983) p. 238-239.
25. Please see Hippolyte Adolph Taine, *Twentieth Century Criticism* (ed.) for further detail.
26. Pandey, Manager. *Ibid.*, p. 123.
27. *Ibid.*
28. Klarer, Mario. *An Introduction to Literary Studies* (London: Routledge, 1999) p. 81-85.
29. Erlich, Victor. *Russian Formalism: History-Doctrine* (London: Yale University Press, 1981) p. 172 quoted in Mario Klarer, *Ibid.*, p. 81-85.
30. Klarer, Mario. *Ibid.*,
31. Goldmann, Lucien. *Method in the Sociology of Literature*, Translated and edited by William Q. Boelhower (Oxford: Basil Blackwell, 1981) p. 19.
32. Eagleton, Terry. *Marxism and Literary Criticism* (London: Methuen & Co Ltd, 1976) p. 32.
33. Goldmann, Lucien. *Ibid.*
34. Eagaleton, Terry. *Ibid.*
35. *Ibid.*, p. 33-34.
36. Boelhower, William Q. Translated and edited Goldmann's *Method in the Sociology of Literature* (Oxford: Basil Blackwell, 1981) p. 8.
37. Williams, Raymond. Keywords, *Ibid.*, p. 84-85.

38. Eagaleton, Terry. *Ibid.*, p. 2.
39. *Ibid.*, p. 3.
40. Quoted in Terry Eagaleton. *Ibid.*, p. 4.
41. *Ibid.*
42. *Ibid.* p. 10.
43. Fischer, Ernst, *Art Against Ideology* (1969) quoted in Terry Eagaleton. *Ibid.*, p. 17.
44. Quoted in Terry Eagaleton. *Ibid.*, p. 18.
45. Terry Eagleton. *Ibid.*, p. 21.
46. Fox, Ralph. *The Novel and the People* (1937) quoted in Terry Eagaleton. *Ibid.*, p. 23.
47. Quoted in Terry Eagleton. *Ibid.*, p. 26.
48. *Ibid.*, p. 28.
49. *Ibid.*, p. 28.
50. *Ibid.*, p. 29.
51. Williams, Raymond. *Marxism and Literature. Ibid.*, p. 46.
52. *Ibid.*, p. 45-54.
53. *Ibid.*, p. 52.
54. *Ibid.*, p. 54.
55. Zelliot, Eleanor. *Ibid.*, p. 269-270.
56. *Ibid.*, p. 275.
57. *Ibid.*, p. 275.
58. Quoted in Eleanor Zelliot. *Ibid.*, p. 280-281.
59. Zelliot, Eleanor. *Ibid.*, p. 281.
60. *Ibid.*
61. Quoted in Sharan Kumar Limbale. Dalit Sahitya Ka Saundryashastra (Delhi: Vani Prakashan, 2000) p. 11.
62. Gooptu, Nandini. *'Caste, Deprivation and Politics: the Untouchables in U.P. Towns in the Early Twentieth Century'* in Peter Robb (ed.) Dalit Movement and the Meaning of Labor in India (Delhi: Oxford University Press, 1993) p. 286.
63. *Ibid.*, p. 290.
64. *Ibid.*, p. 291.
65. Quoted in Ramnika Gupta (ed.) *Dalit Chetna: Soch* (Hazaribagh: Navlakhan Prakashan, 1998) p. 33.
66. *Ibid.*
67. Please see Sharan Kumar Limbale. *Ibid.* for further detail.
68. Ram, Nandu. *Beyond Ambedkar: Essays on Dalits in India* (Delhi: Har-Anand, 1995) p. 31.

3

Dalit Consciousness and Movement

The very first question that comes to our mind while studying *Dalit* Liberation Movement is as to who is a *Dalit*? The confusion centres on the connotations of the word '*Dalit*' which was originally used as a Marathi and Hindi translation of the British term 'Depressed Classes'. There are varieties of nomenclatures such as Untouchables, *Harijan*s, Depressed Classes, *Dalits*, Servile Classes, Weaker Sections, *Panchamas*, *Atishudras*, *Avarnas*, *Antyajas* and Scheduled Castes. The term 'Depressed Classes' refer to those castes, which belong to the lowest rung of the Hindu caste hierarchy and whose touch and proximity is considered as polluting by the Caste Hindus. This was a British innovation from an article written by Dr. Annie Besant in the Indian Review, February 1909 with the caption 'The Uplift of the Depressed Classes'[1]. Further, the term 'Depressed Classes' was mentioned in the Census Report 1921, but the castes constituting the 'Depressed Classes' were not defined. The term 'Depressed Classes' was used before 1930, but since the enactment of the Government of India Act 1935, they are consistently referred to as 'Scheduled Castes'.

In 1901, Risely, the then Census Commissioner of India, attempted to classify the Hindu castes. The term 'Scheduled Castes' appeared for the first time in the Government of India Act 1935. The Simon Commission coined this term in 1928; later on, the British Government issued the Government of India (Scheduled Castes) Order 1936, specifying certain castes and tribes. This category of the Scheduled Castes was also known as *Harijan*s, *i.e.*, Children of God-a term coined by Narasimha Mehta and adopted by Mahatma Gandhi in 1933. Some leaders of the castes consider *Harijan* nomenclature pejorative and they prefer to be called as '*Dalits*' *i.e.*, the oppressed.

The word *Dalit* is referred to broken, ground down trodden people who become subject to deliberate act of exploitation by those above them in a hierarchical social system. The *Dalit* Panthers, once a militant organization, had used the term in its Manifesto. It says, "Members of Scheduled Castes and Scheduled Tribes, neo-Buddhists, the working people, the landless poor peasants, women and those who are being exploited politically, economically and in the name of religion are called *Dalits*"[2]. It further elucidates, "We do not want a little place in *Brahaman* Alley. We want the rule of the whole land. We are not looking at persons by a system. Change of heart, liberal education, etc. will not end our state of exploitation. When we gather a revolutionary mass, rouse the people, out of the struggle of this giant mass will come the tidal wave of revolution"[3].

Thus, "the Untouchables of India had themselves chosen 'a new identity', 'a revised self image' that of *Dalit* to indicate their lack of belief in being polluting, their sense that their condition was the fault of the caste system, and their inclusion in the Ambedkar movement of all those subordinated by their religions, social and economic status."[4] Through this 'new identity', *Dalit* Movement directed itself "towards status-improvement *vis-à-vis* social mobility among *Dalits* and shaping their agitational sensitivity and assertion for achieving their rights of equality and equal opportunity, self-respect and a respectful identity."[5]

Thus the Marathi word '*Dalit*' was chosen by the community itself and is used proudly; and even in the English Press, this word is being used without translation. "None of the normal words Untouchable, Scheduled Castes, Depressed Classes, Gandhi's euphemism, *Harijan*—had the same connotation. *Dalit* implies those who have been broken, ground down by those above them in a deliberate and active way. There is in the word itself an inherent denial of pollution, *Karma*, and justified caste hierarchy."[6] Professor Gangadhar Pantawane, founder-editor of *Asmitadarsh* (Mirror of Identity), the chief organ of *Dalit* literature, defines the word as follows, "To me *Dalit* is not a caste. He is a man exploited by the social and economic traditions of this country. He does not believe in God, Rebirth, Soul, and Holy Books teaching separatism, Fate and Heaven because they have made him a slave. He does believe in humanism. *Dalit* is a symbol of change and revolution."[7]

These are the changing perceptions about the community, which was subjected to 'institutionalized deprivation' for centuries and its struggle for Liberation. It started with very reformative kind of attitudes and passed through several radical and revolutionary phases. There were dynamic changes occurred at definitional level of the movement and today in socio-political system the word '*Dalit*' is widely acceptable and used. But, not much of elucidation is available about the introduction of the term 'Scheduled Castes' either in the Constitution or in any laws or rules. It was in 1901 that the then Census Commissioner of India, Risley tried for the first time to classify the Hindu castes. Then in 1911 an enquiry was made to identify which of the castes and tribes were discriminated against on religious and social grounds. In 1921, these castes and tribes were called the 'Depressed Classes' and J.H. Hutton, the then Census Commissioner, systematically categorized the Depressed Classes.

The expression of the term 'Scheduled Castes' first was coined by the Simon Commission and was placed in the Government of India Act 1935. Prior to this Act, they were known as Untouchables, Depressed Classes or exterior castes. In April 1936, the Government of India (Scheduled Castes) Order issued by British Government specified certain castes, races, and tribes as Scheduled Castes in different provinces of India and the list was continuation of the earlier list of depressed Classes. Further, the list drawn in the Constitution of India (1950) was a revised version of the above-mentioned Order of 1936. The test applied was the social, educational and economic backwardness arising out of the historical customs of Untouchability. Certain specific provisions were made to fulfil the assurance of 'Justice, social, economic and political' that has been held out by the Preamble of the Constitution.

There is no definition of Scheduled Castes and Tribes in the Constitution itself. But the President is empowered to draw up a list in consultation with the Governor of each States, subject to revision by Parliament (Articles 341-342). Here it is proper to mention about the Constitutional provisions with reference to Scheduled Castes.

In the Preamble[8] itself we have the pledge to secure to all citizens:

- Justice, social, economic and political;
- Liberty of thought, expression, belief, faith of worship;
- Equality of status and opportunity

whereby the concept of disabilities arising out of the practice of Untouchability in earlier period find no place. Then, there are various Articles safeguarding the Scheduled Castes, like Articles 15, 16, 17, 19, 23, 25, 29, 38, 46, 164, 330, 334, 335, 338, 341, and 366. Further, the Parliament passed the Untouchability Offence Act (UOA) to make the practice of Untouchability a cognizable offence punishable under the law. This Act came into operation in December 1956 and was amended in September 1976, and is known as 'Protection of Civil Rights Act' (PCRA). Thus Untouchability is legally no longer existent though many still bear stigma of the past in social sphere.

We find a long history of struggle for *Dalit* Liberation where they have gone for conscious attempt to redefine their self-image and many dynamic and landmark changes have occurred at the definitional level during the course of the movement. Today the word *Dalit* is widely acceptable and used all over the country; many social scientists have started referring to the *Dalits* and ex-Untouchables or the Scheduled Castes inter-changeably. We have also used the term *Dalit*, in this work, for the ex-Untouchables or the Scheduled Castes who by articulating their self-realization and their struggle against the caste oppression and by their "will to act against exploitation, a rise from oppression, from death to life, from darkness to light"[9] are continuing their Movement.

An understanding of the development of term '*Dalit*' itself reflects changing nature of the community and provides meaningful insights to analyse the nature and scope of *Dalit* consciousness. In fact, *Dalit* consciousness is the political consciousness that is expressed politically during the course of the *Dalit* movement. Political consciousness is a complex concept, as we discussed in the second chapter, and it is a very comprehensive concept playing a 'catalyst role' in the articulation of *Dalit* community. It is participative having significant impact on the political system and its actors, both subjectively and objectively. It connotes self-image *vis-à-vis* other individuals and communities, their relationship with socio-political locations and their linkages/connectivity with socio-eco-political and cultural structures of society. Political consciousness characterizes an individual's or community's cognitive comprehensibility of its objective conditions as well as its subjective awareness that, in turn, forms through social experiences, political struggles and cultural traits.

To understand *Dalit* consciousness is a complex process as it incorporates several complexities like political consciousness. It includes the understanding of the *Dalits* politics, processes of political socialization and political culture among *Dalits*, its impact on the construction of political consciousness and its different ways of expressions including literature. An effort has been made to understand *Dalit* movement in India in the following section along with the understanding of *Dalit* aesthetics.

Dalit consciousness is guided by the Ambedkarite ideology, programmes, leadership and organization and incorporates both institutionalised and non-institutionalised individual and collective actions initiated and adopted by the community to achieve desired goals. Leadership provided by Dr. B.R. Ambedkar had powerful impact on the community and subsequent course of *Dalit* movement draws inspiration and strength from his vision. We would discuss his impact on the *Dalit* movement in the next section.

Political consciousness is informed through the multiple factors: level of political education, articulated political opinion, amount and quantum of suppression, marginalization of a particular community, urge for radical changes and many more. It is to be noted that the greater amount of political consciousness would increase and enlarge the level of political participation. It would be observed, in the course of this study, that the greater amount of articulated political consciousness among the *Dalit* community has increased and broadened the level and scope of political participation, particularly since Dr. Ambedkar through out the country. In fact, there exists a proliferation of consciousness that is felt politically and expressed among the *Dalit* community.

We can identify a progressive pattern in the expression of political consciousness which is formed through processes of political socialization, political participation and political culture, thus, making it 'a functional catalyst' providing general participation orientations, community mobilization and identity building processes. We have identified in the last chapter that political consciousness performs the following tasks

1. Subjective understanding of the self;
2. Transmission of knowledge from one generation to another;

3. Objective cognition of the socio-eco-politico-cultural conditions;
4. Critical relationship with other communities and the structures of powers and economic controls; and
5. Transforming society consciously with a visionary movement.

Accordingly, we find that a new self-image with overall general political participation is being cultivated by *Dalits* through assertion of their rights and continuation of their movement for social change and for the establishment of an egalitarian society.

Meaning of the term 'Movement'

Here it is pertinent to narrate a brief history of *Dalit* movement in India and its relationship with the literary criticism. We will start this section with the very definition of the term 'Movement'.

We find various concepts such as 'social movement', 'revolt', 'agitation', 'political action', 'collective action', 'reform' and 'revolution', which have major thrust to bring about changes in socio-political system. But it needs a serious attention to define these terms, particularly, the term 'movement' with special reference to *Dalits*.

There is no precise definition of the term 'social movement' accepted by scholars of different disciplines or even scholars belonging to the same discipline. "Like many other terms, such as, 'democracy', 'masses', 'popular', 'equality', the term 'movement' is often used differently by different social activists, political leaders and scholars. Some scholars use the term 'movement' interchangeably with 'organization' or 'union'. Some use it to mean a historical trend or tendency. It is fashionable for political leaders and social reformer to call their activities 'movement' even though their activities are confined to the forming of organizations with less than a dozen members. Some claim to launch movements by issuing press statements on public issues. Like many other words, the term 'movement' is still regarded a 'Hurrah'! word to use T.D. Weldon's memorable classification."[10]

It was during early nineteenth century that the term 'social movement' gained currency in Europe. This was the period of social upheaval and change where political leaders and authors were concerned with emancipation of the exploited classes. But there was not a consistent definition of the term 'movement', and it was during second quarter of the last century that attempts were made to define the concept of social movement. We will discuss some of the related concepts before going into details of the term 'social movement.' One of the most important terms synonymous to movement is Collective action that may be of two kinds:

(*a*) Institutionalised collective action
(*b*) Non-institutionalised collective action

"The action that is legally permitted and 'widely accepted as binding in society or part of society' at a given point of time is institutionalised action. Such action includes petitioning, voting in elections, and fighting legal battles in courts of law...Non-institutionalised collective action takes several forms, such as, protest, agitation, strike, *Satyagraha*, *Hartal*, *Gherao* and riot. Agitations or protests are not strictly speaking social movement, though a social movement develops in course of time, and it beings with protest or agitation, which may not have the 'organization' or 'ideology' for change."[11]

Ghanshyam Shah[12] classifies movements as revolt, rebellion, reform and revolution to bring about changes in the political system. Reform does not challenge political system *per se*. It attempts to bring about changes in the relations between the parts of the system in order to make it more efficient, responsive and workable. A revolt is a challenge to political authority, aimed at overthrowing the government. A rebellion is an attack on existing authority without any intention of seizing power. In a revolution, a section of society launch an organized struggle to overthrow not only the established government and regime but also the socio economic structure which sustains it and replace the structure by an alternative social order.

According to the Marxist scholars, the causes for social movement could be identified in the economic structure of society. Antagonistic interests between the propertied and labour classes are inherent in the class-based society, which generates contradictions. Subaltern studies group has begun to study 'history from below', emphasized on cultural factors, and also viewed a linear development of class-consciousness. As per the Marxist ideology, the propertied classes in a class-based society use the coercive power of the State, as well as of the other institutions, including religion, education, mass media, to expose their ideology of society and to control the exploited classes, whereas the labour classes resist, protest and occasionally revolt or launch organized and collective action against the dominance of the propertied classes. It is their effort to bring about revolutionary political change by overthrowing the dominant classes in power. Though to Marxists structural causes of conflicting economic interests are central to their studies, a number of Marxist scholars have begun to pay attention to ethnic, religious and other cultural factors. Some of them have attempted to analyse the nature of the consciousness of the exploited classes.

Further Ghanshyam Shah[13] noticed that there is another line of argument which asserts that mass movement or protest are redundant in the perspective of Indian culture and civilization due to its 'miltilinear character' and all 'pervasive hierarchy'. Because of the *Brahmanical* ideology and hierarchical social structure the oppressed classes have become docile, obedient and fatalist. But scholars who point to a number of struggles by the oppressed classes in pre and post Independence India refute such assertions. Some explain these protests as a result of the conflict between 'tradition' and 'modernity'. According to them parliamentary democracy has been transplanted in India, where there is no tradition of voluntary effort. People have developed an ambivalent attitude towards authority, they take advantages offered by the political authority but at the same time do not legitimise it.

Morris-Jones argues, "Even after Independence government is relied upon and at the same time spat upon and abused. The same man who is looking to government one moment may in the next take part in demonstrations involving violence and on a scale that threatens to make any government impossible."[14] This is the outcome of the constant conflict between traditional values and modern institutions.

According to Rajni Kothari, democracy in India has become a playground for growing corruption, criminalization, repression and intimidation of large masses of the people. The role of the State in 'social transformation' has been undermined. People have started asserting their rights through various struggles: "There is discontent and despair in the air still highly diffuse, fragmented and unorganised. But there is growing awareness of rights, felt politically and expressed politically, and by and large still aimed at the state. Whenever a mechanism of mobilization has become available, this consciousness has often found expression against very odds, against a constellation of interests that are too powerful and complacent to shed (even share) the privileges. At bottom it is consciousness against a paradigm of society that rests on deliberate indifference to the plight of impoverished and destitute who are being driven to the threshold of starvation by the logic of paradigm itself."[15]

Kothari feels that mass mobilization, at the grassroots level, is both necessary and desirable. He asserts that it is in the state of "vacuum in the traditional superstructure of the liberal polity that was supposed to render it humane despite powerful trends that the real counter trends are to be found not in the party system, not in the area of electoral politics and of State power, not in the typical confrontation between the so-called haves and have-nots within the conventional economic space dominated by trade unions. In their place there is emerging a new arena of counteraction, of countervailing tendencies, of counter-cultural movements and more generally of counter-challenge to existing paradigms of thought and action."[16]

Thus, after analysing the above typologies, it is evident that to define a social movement is a difficult and complex task. However, a working definition of the social movement is necessary to examine the *Dalit* movement. Paul Wilkinson gives the following working concept of 'social movement': "A social movement is a deliberative collective endeavour to promote change in any direction and by any means, not excluding violence illegality, revolution or withdrawal into utopian community. Social movements are thus clearly different from historical movements, tendencies or trends. It is important to note, however, that such tendencies and trends, and the influence of the unconscious and irrational factors in human behaviour, may be of crucial importance in illuminating the problems of interpreting of explaining social movements. A social movement must evince a minimal degree and organization though this may range form a loose, informal or partial level of organization to the highly institutionalised and bureaucratised movements and the corporate group. A social movement's commitment to change and the raison d'être of its organization are founded upon the conscious volition, normative commitment to the movement's aims or beliefs, and active participation on the part of the followers or members."[17]

There is some consensus among the scholars regarding element of volition and normative commitment. For instance, "Heberle conceives of these belief systems, as an expression of the collective will of the people among whom they are accepted. He is emphatic that it is the element of volition that makes the beliefs socially effective. It is the conscious volition of individuals acting collectively that brings about the embodiment of ideologies in social movements."[18]

Thus major ingredients of social movement consist of objectives, ideology, programmes, leadership and organization, which are co-ordinated and are inter-dependent. We will examine the *Dalit* movement with the above working concept of the social movement where efforts are to seriously examine the important components and their effect on the *Dalit* movement in its search for 'new self-image' and new identity-building process.

Brief History of *Dalit* Movement

The third issue, which needs attention, is that of the beginning of the *Dalit* movement. This is also a complex issue and there are many contending views where some scholars trace the beginning right from the *Bhakti* movement or even to earlier period while many others consider the Mahar movement in Maharashtra as an important milestone of the movement. There is evident a consensus among scholars that *Dalit* struggle during the colonial period, particularly after the arrival of Dr. B.R. Ambedkar, gained momentum where the main issues were gaining recognition, representation and power within the changing political order.

We will trace a brief history of the *Dalit* movement dealing with the important issues raised during the course of the movement and finally with the identity building process. Ghanshyam Shah[19] has classified *Dalit* movement into two broad categories, *viz.*,

(*a*) Reformative Movement; and
(*b*) Alternative Movement.

Whereas the Reformative movement attempted to reform the caste system to resolve problem of Untouchability and the Alternative movement makes an effort to create an alternative socio-cultural structure where caste domination is eliminated and social justice is ensured to every person with a dignified human life. The Reformative movements are further sub-divided into the following categories:

(*i*) *Bhakti* Movement;
(*ii*) Neo-*Vedantic* Movement; and
(*iii*) *Sanskritisation* Movement.

The Alternative movements are also sub-divided into the following:

(*i*) Proselytization Movement; and
(*ii*) Secular Movement.

Bhakti Movement (12th to 18th centuries) attempted to purify Hinduism of its evils and fought against the tyranny of Caste System. This movement, after the Buddhism, left a great appeal for the establishment of an egalitarian society and produced saints like Chokhamela and Eknath[20], whose poetry become instrumental in the *Dalit* awakening. Both of them offered models for change in regard to Untouchability. The lives of both are known by legend; devotees on the pilgrimages and in *Bhajan* sessions sing their songs. Chokhamela was a Mahar, the only important *Bhakti* figure in Maharashtra from an Untouchable caste. Eknath was a *Brahman* from the holy city of Paithan who wrote about Chokhamela, ate with Maharas, allowed Untouchables into his *Bhajan* sessions and wrote poems in the persona of a Mahar who was wiser in spiritual matters than the Brahmans.

Saint Chokhamela was born in the second half of the thirteenth century, probably about the time that Dyaneshwar, who is considered the founder of the *Bhakti* sect in Maharashtra, was born. He died in 1338 in Mangalvedhe, a town in Sholapur district. Chokhamela and his family seem to have followed the traditional duties of a Mahar.

There is an inherent element of protest against the concept of Untouchability in Chokhamela's *Bhakti* songs, though his songs also reveal the traditional devotion and piety of the *Bhakta*. Chokhamela questioned the very basis of the caste system, which preached purity:

> The only impurity is in the five elements.
> There is only one substance in the world.
> Then who is pure and who is impure?
> The cause of pollution is the creation of the body.
> In the beginning, at the end, there is nothing but pollution.
> No one knows anyone who was born pure.
> Chokha says, in wonder, who is pure?[21]
> *Abhanga* 11 in *Chokhamela Abhang Gatha*, 1950

The central argument of Chokhamela's poetry was protest and questioning supremacy of the *Brahmanical* order, though he lived in his traditional role as a Mahar with its traditional limitations. The spirit of most of the *abhangas* is delight in the Lord, delivery from life's sufferings through devotion. Even though agony is there, the central message is that Chokha, even though a Mahar, could experience the grace of God.

Next important figure of the *Bhakti* Movement is Shri Eknath Maharaj (C.1533-1599) whose background was completely different from that of Chokhamela. He belonged to a Brahman family of considerable fame and the political world around Eknath was also dissimilar to the fourteenth century world in which Chokhamela lived. Chokhamela was probably a young man when Alla-ud-din-Khilji stormed Devagiri in 1296; his time also witnessed the raids of Muhammad Tuglaq, who shifted his capital to Daulatabad in 1327, but Chokhamela died before the stable Bahmani kingdom was created in 1347. It is also noticeable that the political references are missing in Chokhamela's works. But Eknath lived at the time of the Ahmadnagar Sultanate, whose influence can be seen in the number of Persian words that Eknath used in his writings, in the Muslim terms for administration, which he wove into the poetry, which used obligations to government as an analogy for debts to God.

Eknath's most important contribution of *Bhakti* tradition is for the Untouchables. He wrote some three hundred *bharuds*, drama and poems meant to be acted out and of these almost fifty are written as if an Untouchable were the author. Forty-seven *bharuds* seem to come from the mouth of Mahar men or women; one is written in the name of Mang, one of the three important Untouchable castes.

The poems in which the Mahar is the speaker are *Johar* poems, beginning with the greetings used by Mahars to their superiors. Most are very different from the poems of Chokhamela; in Eknath's *bharuds*, the Mahar not only preaches about morality to others, the necessity of a *Guru* and the company of the *Sants*, but also of the calamity of the rebirth that is inevitable for those who do not follow the *Bhakti* path, and of the false lives of the pseudo-pious.

Eknath's writings make it clear that there is no caste distinction in the eyes of God, as he puts in the following song:

> God baked pots with Gora,
> drove cattle with Chokha,
> cut grass with Savata Mali,
> wore garments with Kabir,
> coloured hide with Ravidas,
> sold meat with butcher Sajana,
> melted gold with Narahari,
> carried cow-dung with Janabai,
> and even become the Mahar messenger of Damaji.[22]

Thus, with the growth of nationalism and the awakening interest in the upliftment of the depressed classes, *Bhakti* movement, still very much alive, came to serve a new purpose. Mahadeo Govind Ranade, a member of the reformist religious group, the Prarthana Samaj, as well as a leading nationalist, wrote in 1900 of the historic importance of the *Bhakti* movement: "like the Protestant Reformation in Europe in the sixteenth century, there was a Religious, Social and Literary Revival and Reformation in India. This Religious Revival was not *Brahamanical* in its orthodoxy; it was heterodox in its spirit of protest against forms and ceremonies and class distinctions based on birth, and ethical in its preference of a pure heart, and of the law of love, to all other acquired merits and good works. This Religious Revival was the work of the people, of the masses, and not of the classes. At its head were Saints and Prophets, Poets and Philosophers, who sprang chiefly from the lower orders of society—tailors, carpenters, potters, gardeners, shop-keepers, barbers, and even Mahars—more often than Brahmans."[23]

In Northern India, there was *Bhakti* resurgence from the late nineteenth century. In this period Untouchable ideologues, who spearheaded social movements against caste distinctions, challenged, in particular, social division of labour based on ritual status-this, they argued, prevented occupational diversification and in turn precipitated material deprivations, powerlessness and lack of education. In the early twentieth century, adherence to *Bhakti* tradition and veneration of Kabir and Ravidas became widespread among the Untouchables in Uttar Pradesh. We will discuss, in detail, the social context of *Bhakti* resurgence in this work.

After *Bhakti* Movement, Neo-*Vedantic* Movement attempted a re-interpretation of the doctrine of Hinduism so as to cleanse it of its evils and render it back to the original priestly purity. Exponents, like Dayanand and Vivekanand, played an important role during this period. These movements attempted to remove Untouchability by taking them into the fold of the Caste System. According to the pioneers of these movements, Untouchability was not an essential part of Hinduism, and for that matter, of the Caste System.

Dayanand Saraswati, the founder of the Arya Samaj, believed that the Caste System was a political institution created by the rulers. He said, "in fact, any *Brahman*, who is disqualified for his work, becomes at once a *Sudra de jure* and a *Sudra*, who qualifies for it becomes at once a *Brahman de jure*."[24] The Arya Samaj started various educational and welfare programmes for the upliftment of the Scheduled Castes.

Satish Kumar Sharma's book Social Movement and Social Change (1985) is an important study, which examines the relationship between the Arya Samaj and the Untouchables. The study is confined to Punjab only but some of his observations are also applicable for the other parts of the country. Sharma observes that Arya Samaj was against the political movements of the Untouchables. It went against any move initiated by the Untouchables for their solidarity and integration.

Thus seen, the neo-*Vedantic* and non-*Brahman* movements played "an important catalystic role"[25] in developing anti-caste or anti-Hinduism *Dalit* movement in the country. The Satyashodhak Samaj and the Self Respect movements in Maharashtra and Tamil Nadu, the *Adi-Dharma* and *Adi-Andhra* movements in Bengal and Uttar Pradesh, are important anti-Untouchability movements, which were launched, in the last quarter of the nineteenth and early part of this century. We also get scattered references on the Adi-Hindu and Namashudra movements.

Mark Juergensmeyer's book Religion as Social Vision (1982) deals with the *Adi-Dharma* movement against Untouchability in twentieth century Punjab. It began in 1920s. The main plea of the movement was that the Untouchables constituted a *quam*, and their *quam* existed in India from time immemorial, *i.e.*, before the Hindu arrived. According to Mark Juergensmeyer, "It had established a fact which previously had been unproved: that the Untouchable castes were capable of mobilizing for their own benefits, and of organizing in ways that permitted them to compete under the conditions that governed the socio-political area at large."[26] Later on, the movement was absorbed in Ambedkar's Scheduled Castes Federation.

Through *Sanskritization* movement, a section of Untouchables who could improve their economic condition, either by abandoning or continuing their traditional occupations, launched struggle for higher status in the caste hierarchy. The founder of this concept, M.N. Srinivas, defines the concept of *Sanskritization* as follows: "The caste system is far from a rigid system in which the position of each component caste is fixed for all time. Movement has always been possible, and especially so in the middle regions of the hierarchy. A low caste was able, in a generation or two, to rise to a higher position in the hierarchy by adopting vegetarianism or teetotalism, and by *Sanskritizing* its rituals and pantheon. In short, it took over, as far as possible, the customs, rites, and beliefs of the Brahmins and the adoption of the *Brahmanic* way of life by a low caste seems to have been frequent, though theoretically forbidden. This process has been called *Sanskritisation*."[27]

In this way the lower castes followed *Sanskritic* norms and rituals. They tried to justify their claims to a higher social status in the caste hierarchy by inventing suitable mythologies. The Sharars or Nadars of Tamil Nadu have crossed the boundary of Untouchability. The Iravas or Ezhạvas of Kerala have also blurred, if not completely destroyed, the line of Untouchability. The Nadar organised movements in the late nineteenth century against the civic disabilities they suffered. They entered the political system by first supporting the Justice Party in the early 1930s and later the Congress party. They have moved from the lower rungs of the ritual hierarchy to a position of status and power. Similarly, the Ezhavas formed their caste organization in 1903, known as SNDA Yogam (Association for the Maintenance of Dharma founded by Sri Narayana). The Association launched activities for *Sanskritizing* norms and customs of the Iravas. They launched a *Satyagraha* for temple entry in 1920s, as well as bargained with the government for economic opportunities and political positions, thus, improving their status.

It is clear by now that the *Dalit* movement in pre-Independence period had achieved a respectable status. Though reformative in nature, the *Bhakti* movement, the Neo-*Vedantic* and *Sanskritization* movements have contributed meaningfully for the proliferation of political consciousness among *Dalits* and it can be said that these movements laid down firm foundations for the *Dalit* Liberation movement whose agenda include recognition of human existence, social mobility, political participation, social change and establishment of an egalitarian society. Now we will discuss the Alternative movements.

Through Conversion Movement, *Dalits* offer a new alternative religion, Buddhism, in negation of Hinduism. It started with Ambedkar's personal conversion announcement in 1935 which was followed by a Mahar Conference in 1936 where Ambedkar declared:

> Religion is for man; man is not for religion,
> If you want to gain self-respect, change your religion.
> If you want to create a co-operative society change your religion.
> If you want power, change your religion.
> If your want equality, change your religion.
> If you want independence, change your religion.
> If you want to make the world in which you live, happy, change your religion....[28]

Buddhism offered scriptural justification for worth, achieved by mind and action, not by birth. So in 1956, Dr. Ambedkar took *Diksha* from the oldest Buddhist monk in India before a large audience in Nagpur and set in motion the conversion process that brought over three million Indians into the Buddhist fold in the next few years. The Conversion Movement gave new, changed identity, as Professor

Gangadhar Pantavane, stated: "Bhimrao has placed us in the lap of a life giving religion and so has awakened psychological independence. This is the religion of Gautam, who with love won the world, and the spine of this religion is humanity."[29] In this regard, Namdev Dhasal said, "Conversion to Buddhism. freed the Scheduled Castes from mental and psychological enslavement. Religion has an attraction for the common man and it was not easy to change his attitude towards it. The Buddhists have liberated themselves from old ideas of *Karma* and destiny and from worship of Hindu gods. To some extent this facilitated their adopting rational attitudes to their conditions in society, the chance of their actively striving to change their conditions for better."[30]

Thus, the Conversion Movement made an immense appeal to the *Dalits*, though its benefits are mostly limited to mental relax but otherwise impact is remarkable. It rejected Hinduism, and the caste system. But the Conversion has one facet of a multi-level effort: economic improvement of the masses, exploitation free system etc., which was expected come through some other path. The Conversion seems to have helped to create the will to probe every possible means for remaining united and asserting independent identity. It also hailed the vision for an alternate society where all people are equal and enjoy a dignified life.

In the Secular Movements, which include economic issues also, we find an attempt to build an alternative socio-cultural identity for the oppressed classes. During this movement, *Dalit* literature flourished well and people started propagating their ideas by publishing their original writings such as poems, stories, plays which are used as a means of protest against Hindu intellectual tradition, the Hindu religion and Hindu ethics.

There occurred land grab movements in late 1960s where *Dalit* agricultural labourers participated at a number of places in Andhra Pradesh, Tamil Nadu, Karnataka, Kerala, Bihar, Maharashtra and Uttar Pradesh. These movements are still active in numerous villages of the country. They have contributed in generating class-consciousness among the people living in a caste-structured society. These movements are also helping to develop consciousness among the oppressed classes regarding the socio-economic structure and cultural reality, which keep them subjugated.

Thus, all these movements represented "ample evidence of the *Dalit* Movement even prior to the enactment of the 1919 reforms, growing in size and political significance through the 1920s and 1930s. *Dalits* may not have had a single organization parallel to the Muslim League or Hindu Mahasabha, but they did have grassroots organizations, a recognized leadership, pre-eminent among whom Dr. Ambedkar; and a common demand for political recognition, for representation of their own, as well as for dignity, equality and justice."[31]

Study of the awakening of the *Dalits* in the last century can be sub-divided[32] as:

(*a*) Era of struggle for the recognition of human existence and socio-political rights till Independence (1920-1950),
(*b*) Era of restructuring through social mobility and political participation (1950-1985),
(*c*) Era of actual sharing or exercise of power (1985 onwards).

As it is evident from the earlier analysis that long before the era of struggle for recognition of human existence and socio-political rights, attempts were made to emancipate Untouchables from the clutches of upper castes exploitation and degradation by various saints and social reformers. But they tried to do so on the basis of philosophical and religious not political grounds and supported, somehow, continuation of the *Varna* system. Basic challenge to this exploitative system came from the Conversion Movement, which rejected philosophical tenets of the caste system. But reform movements within the Hindu society continued to keep Untouchables at the mercy of good will of the upper castes people. None of them made any attempt to encourage these depressed and distressed people to stand on their own feet and assert, as equal human beings. From this point of view, the *Dalits*, as politically conscious of their rights and privileges, were not able to assert politically, however, some of them did succeed in making upward social mobility. It was only during the Freedom Movement that these castes started to assert in terms of socio-political awakening based on social mobility.

Analysing the periods of the *Dalit* movement of the last century, one finds that the level of socio-cultural awakening and consciousness was raised in the first two decades of the century, and with the arrival of Dr. B.R. Ambedkar, this movement reached its zenith. "The years between 1930 and 1936 were a turning point in the history of the *Dalit* movement in India. These years witnessed the All-India Depressed Classes Conference at Nagpur in 1930; Ambedkar's attendance at the First Round Table Conference; his clash with Gandhi before and at the Second Round Table Conference, culminating in the Poona Pact of 1932; and the famous Conversion announcement in 1935, 'I have been born a Hindu but I will not die a Hindu.'"[33]

The events of this period led to Ambedkar's final disillusionment with Hinduism and with the Congress leadership. At the same time these events revealed the power represented by Ambedkar and *Dalit* movement that had risen with him and confirmed him as an unparalleled leader of the *Dalits*, forcing the Congress leadership to deal with his demands.

Thus, "Dr. Ambedkar played three important roles during his lifetime: that of a caste leader, that of an Untouchable spokesman, and that of national statesman. In his first leadership role, he was guide, *guru* and decision maker for his own caste, the Mahars of Maharashtra, from the mid-twenties of this century until his death. From the early 1930s onwards he was chief spokesman of the Untouchables. In his third role, he spoke on all phases on India's development, worked on problems of labour and law as a member of the Government, and even put aside some of his own theories to help create a viable, generally accepted Constitution."[34]

It was at the time of Simon Commission that Dr. Ambedkar came forward with his demands categorically. He submitted, on the behalf of the Depressed Classes of Bombay, a statement[35] for asking some guarantees before Simon Commission, which are mentioned hereunder:

(*i*) That the education of the depressed classes shall be recognized as the first charge on the revenues of the Province and that an equitable and just proportion of the total grant for education shall be earmarked for the benefit of the depressed classes.

(*ii*) That the right of the depressed classes to unrestricted recruitment in the army, navy and the police shall be recognized without any limitation as to caste.

(*iii*) That for a period or 30 years the rights of the depressed classes for priority in the matter of recruitment to all posts, gazetted as well as non-gazetted, in all civil services shall be recognized.

(*iv*) That the right of the depressed classes to effective representation on the local bodies shall be recognized by the Provincial Government.

(*v*) That the right of the depressed classes to appeal to the Government of India in cases of violation of these rights by the Provincial Government shall be recognized and the Government of India shall be given the power to compel the Provincial Government to conform to the law in these matters.

Thus, it became clear, at the time of the list of the Simon Commission, that *Dalits* were becoming politically conscious and they had started agitation for the recognition of their socio-political rights. During the visit of the Simon Commission, it was announced that after the work of the Commission was over, the representatives of India be assembled for discussion on the future Constitution of India. This was the background of the three Round Table Conferences, which took place in London from 1930-32. Dr. Ambedkar attended the First Round Table Conference along with M.N. Srinivasan of Madras to represent India's Untouchables, he was unequivocal that "Untouchables needed politically power and equally definite that this could only be gained within the framework of an Independent India. He stated: The point of view I'll try to put as briefly as I can. It is this, that the bureaucratic form of Government in India should be replaced by a Government, which will be a Government of the people, by the people and for the people. Arguing that the goodwill of the British is irrelevant, he went on: The Government of India does realize the necessity of removing the social evils, which are eating into, the vitals of Indian society and which have blighted the lives of the downtrodden classes for years. The Government of India does realize that the landlords are squeezing the masses dry and the capitalists are not giving the labourer a living wage and decent conditions of work. Yet it is a most painful thing that it has not dared to touch any of these evils. Why. These are some of the questions raised by the depressed classes. we feel that nobody can remove our grievances as well as we can and we can not remove them unless we get political power in our own hands. No share of this political power can evidently come to us so long as the British government remains as it is. It is only in a *Swaraj* Constitution that we stand any chance of getting the political power in our own hands, without which we cannot bring salvation to our people."[36]

At the Conference, he advocated a unitary state and adult suffrage with reserved seats and safeguards for Untouchables. It is to be noted that it was this Conference that shaped the 1935 Government of India Act; a Federal Constitution in which the Princely States could enter as an autonomous units; a slightly expanded electorate but hardly adult suffrage; and responsible government at the Provincial level highly qualified by residual powers given to British-appointed governors. The Indian National Congress did not attend the First Round Table Conference.

Confrontation between Gandhiji and Dr. Ambedkar became apparent at the second Round Table Conference, when Gandhiji refused to accept separate electorate for the depressed classes and opposed any form of special representation involving reserved seats. Their earlier meeting just before the Second Round Table Conference ended in distress that led negotiations at the Conference difficult. "The situation was exacerbated by Gandhi's questioning of Ambedkar's bona fides: "I say that it is not a proper claim which is registered by Dr. Ambedkar when he seeks to speak for the whole of Untouchables of India. I myself in my own person claim to represent the vast mass of the Untouchables..."[37]

Subsequent declaration of the Communal Award of 1932 by the British Government was responded by Gandhiji in the form of a fast unto death on September 20, 1932, which led to a compromise between Gandhi and Ambedkar, known as the Yerveda or the Poona Pact.

But the differences between Gandhi and Ambedkar surfaced, again, as soon as Gandhi started his League against Untouchability (which was to become *Harijan* Sevak Sangh) and Ambedkar attempted to intervene. There were two important issues: whether the League would be controlled by caste Hindus or the *Dalits* would have have share in control at least, and whether it would only seek to abolish

Untouchability or aim at the abolition of *Chaturvarna* itself. Gandhi firmly held out for caste Hindu control on the grounds that since Untouchability was an evil of Hinduism that had to be purged, Hindus themselves must do this; he also stressed that he was not against *Chaturvarna* as a system. In this way, it became impossible for Gandhi and Ambedkar to work together on the issue of *Dalit* emancipation.

Another important contribution that needs serious attention is the political initiatives taken by Dr. Ambedkar, who was instrumental in establishing three political parties: Independent Labor Party (ILP) in 1936, Scheduled Caste Federation (SCF) in 1942, which led to the formation of the Republican Party of India (RPI) in 1956. These were the attempts to bring Untouchables to larger group or in a solid mass to seek political power. The Programme of the ILP was "mainly to advance the welfare of the labouring classes and the Party accepted with socialist flavour, the principle of state management and state ownership of industries wherever it may become necessary in the interests of the people. Aid to agriculturists through land mortgage banks; co-operative and marketing societies; technical education and the promotion of the new industries; reform of the tenants system; free and compulsory education and a pledge to bring about a fair mixture of caste in the administration were planks of the platform."[38] This Party was able to secure 14 out of 18 seats it contested in the 1937 elections. Eleanor Zelliot writes on this: "With the Conversion announcement in 1935, the establishment of a political party in 1936, and to considerable success in 1937 elections, the shift from attempting to gain status in matters of religion to organizing political activity was nearly complete."[39]

Then, in July 1942, the All-India Depressed Classes Conference was held at Nagpur, which brought the ILP to an end and constituted SCF before a mass of 70,000 of which one third were women. There were two specific demands; one, for separate village settlement of entirely Scheduled Castes villages away from and independent of Hindu villages and the other was renewing the demand for separate electorates. Aside from this, the SCF maintained most of the other specific demands of the ILP. In 1956 Dr. Ambedkar made an attempt to transform the SCF into a party which would speak for all the 'dispossessed' and thus, the RPI was created which, later, put its Charter of Demands[40] in details, some of the demands are as follows:

1. A portrait Dr. B.R. Ambedkar as Father of the Indian Constitution in the Central Hall of the Parliament;
2. The Nation's land given to the landless tiller;
3. Idle and wasteland given to landless labour;
4. Full implementation of the Minimum Wages Act, 1948;
5. Extension of Scheduled Castes privileges to the SCs members who have embraced Buddhism; and
6. Full justice under the Untouchability Offence Act.

Thus, Ambedkar's contribution to the *Dalit* movement becomes its guidtebing force. His was a committed personality for the emancipation of *Dalits* in particular and for the nation-building and social transformation in general. His writings are full of serious analysis of the caste-ridden Indian society and of the Hindu social system. He also gave the most desired direction for modernization and development by framing the Constitution of Free India and served as the first Indian Law Minister for sometimes in the Nehru Cabinet. Finally, he offered an alternative vision of religion by embracing Buddhism.

Now it becomes important to deal with several pertinent questions of *Dalit* movement in continuity. Here our endeavour will be to find out *Dalits* as a category of caste, class and religion, thereafter to recognize the important trends in the *Dalit* movement. First of all, we will discuss *Dalits* as a category of Caste.

Caste is the most striking feature of the Indian society and every one recognizes that Caste System determines the very texture of Indian politics. It has become part and parcel of the Indian Political System. Caste is "a hereditary, endogamous, usually localized group, having a traditional association with an occupation, and a particular position in hierarchy of castes. Relations between castes are governed, among other things, by the concepts of pollution and purity, and generally, maximum commensality occurs within the caste."[41] Castes have come out of ancient fourfold classification of society known as *Varna* scheme which justified the Caste Order on three grounds: the first is what may be called the secular aspect which includes the governmental aspect (Caste Councils, village arbitration procedures and so on) and the political aspects (within caste and inter-caste authority and status alignments). Second, there is the integration aspect. The Caste System not only determines the individual's social station on the basis of group to which he is born but also differentiates and assigns occupational and economic roles. It thus gives a place to every individual from the highest to the lowest and makes for a high degree of identification and integration. Third, there is the aspect of consciousness, which leads to variation of *Varna* according to one's level of understanding of the social system as a whole.

After analysing brief history of the *Dalit* movement, we can say that this movement started as non-*Brahman* movement, which led to anti-caste movement during the *Bhakti* period. It also attempted to purify Hinduism of its evils and fought against the tyranny of the Caste System. This anti-caste movement was, in turn, a part of a broader revolutionary movement that included the National Movement and the Communist and socialist led working class and peasants movements as well. Thus, the *Dalit* movement initiated struggle against the evils of the Caste System, broadened its horizons, addressed to, and affiliated with the working class and peasant struggles.

Coming to the next category of *Dalits* as a class, we find some important observations of the caste-class analysis. Sometimes, there is overlapping of the two social differentiations. One, based on caste is the legacy of the past that has been carried over the present to times. The other is the class differentiation, based on the development of productive forces and the commensurating production relations. Inevitably, the second is growing more powerful each day, and is breaking up the rigid framework imposed by the Caste System. Objective developments are strengthening class divisions and antagonisms and the struggle between the classes is becoming sharper. It is well established that caste based associations can no longer improve the social conditions whereas class consciousness and class struggle unite all sections of the exploited masses against their exploiters, while caste consciousness and caste struggle divide the exploited masses according to their castes while claiming to fight the exploiters. Building a counter-caste ideology of the lower or backward castes cannot fight the caste ideology of the dominant castes. The *Dalit* movement can achieve significant success where it will polarize itself on the class line and will associate itself with the larger struggles outside the caste framework.

The next category that needs attention is that of religion *vis-à-vis Dalits*. Hinduism, because of its several oppressive practices, which have infiltrated pains and atrocities on *Dalits,* was rejected by them. They embraced Buddhism as it preaches egalitarianism and thus *Dalit,* "liberated themselves from old ideas of *Karma*, destiny and from worship of Hindu gods."[42] It was the Conversion movement, announced by Ambedkar in 1936 that "galvanized *Dalits* through out India and it was the choice of Buddhism that lay down the challenge for an alternative Indian identity."[43]

On the basis of this historical analysis, various scholars have identified some important trends of the Dalit Movement in India:

The *Dalit* Movement, in the beginning, was a Reformative movement, which attempted to purify Hinduism of its evils, and fought against the tyranny of the Caste System. During this period, saints like Chokhamela, Eknath, Kabir and Ravidas played a very important role in the awakening of *Dalit* consciousness. Second, with this Reformative movement, there were Alternative movements too, which attempted to create an alternative socio-cultural structure where caste domination is eliminated and every person can live with self-dignity. Third, the *Dalit* Movement did not emerge only in Maharashtra as a result of Ambedkar's leadership, there were similar trend, though of varying degree of strength, in all regions of Indian society. Fourth, the Movement was genuinely anti-caste and not merely a caste reform movement. Internal reforms, like giving up drinking and rejecting customs, which marked the caste as 'low' in a *Brahmanic* hierarchy, were themes everywhere, along with demands of education and entry into employment and political institutions. Fifth, *Dalits* as exploited workers, peasants and agricultural labourers were involved with economic or class issues everywhere, and these were expressed in demands, like land grab movement, made in all regions. Sixth, *Dalit* Movement emerged as a great political force but much weaker in organizational strength and financial resources. Seventh, the *Dalit* Movement had come up with new identity, rejecting Hinduism and embracing Buddhism to build an alternative equitable and egalitarian society. Finally, "Untouchables of India had themselves chosen a new identity, that of *Dalits* to indicate their lack of belief in being polluting, their sense that their condition was the fault of the caste system and their inclusion in the Ambedkar movement."[44] It is also evident that in the course of the Movement the connotation of the word '*Dalit'* is broadened and now it is not confined only to the 'ex-

Untouchables' but it refers to those also who are deprived of their socio-economic and cultural rights.

To understand contemporary *Dalit* struggle two approaches seem to predominate. One is that represented by Professor Nandu Ram who sees three types of contemporary *Dalit* Movements: "Movements against socio-economic exploitation and numerous types of atrocities committed on the *Dalits*; movements for better access to the opportunities and for the realization of goals of equality, liberty, fraternity and justice; and finally movements for gaining self-respect and dignified social identity."[45]

The second approach seeks an underlying unity beneath this diversity, as represented by Rajni Kothari: "The *Dalits*' expectations and strategy seem to be designed to challenge the dominant castes by means of education, employment and special rights, in short, a struggle against the system that begins with challenging injustices within it, thinking of a struggle against 'domination' and imperialism. Or as some of them would say, redefine nature of imperialism in essentially social terms both locally and globally."[46]

Thus, in the post-Independence India, it is urgently needed that political context of the movement be clearly underlined. "At the time of Independence and after, *Dalits* have not become power holders themselves, the movement was not controlling events, and it was suffering a process of co-optation and incorporation. Repression continued and still is continuing which is evident and open and brutal in the villages, but it was overlaid in the co-optation, the winning over with the individuals with few crumbs and the erosion of movement organizations, accompanied by the overflowing paternalistic and benign rhetoric of the party which Ambedkar had described as the party of 'Brahmans and the bourgeois."[47]

Then, what seems the possible path to liberation? Dr. Ambedkar, in one of his works titled 'What Path to Liberation' had argued that a "necessary condition was to overthrow of 'Hindu religious-ideological hegemony'. He had tended to see economic and social oppression as separate structures, taking up cultural change as the way to challenge Hinduism; socialism as the way to overcome exploitation"[48] and a combined struggle, dealing with economic and socio-cultural issues is always needed. Today, this combined struggle is needed more than ever.

Dalit Literature and Aesthetics

The above analysis provides a working framework that manifests interrelations between literary expression and political consciousness among the *Dalits*. We have discussed in the last chapter the nature and scope of literary expression and political consciousness in the community. It is evident that *Dalit* literature is a powerful medium of expression that keeps *Dalit* movement sustaining and provides an untiring zeal.

There are different views regarding the *Dalit* literature, most prominent among them is its critique that *Dalit* literature is a political literature. Of course, the *Dalit* literature is a political literature and it needs to be reaffirmed that the term *Dalit* itself is political identity representing the very denial of the Caste System. According the Prof. Tulsi Ram, "if we examine literature anywhere in the world critically, it would be self-explained that literary expressions represent contemporary political reality and has both: pro and against voices. There is a very close relationship of literature and politics and it is not confined to the expression of *Dalit* literature. For instance, literature written during the Vedic period is called religious literature but, in fact, that represents the political system of the Vedic Age..."[49] In this way, literature becomes political which expresses contemporary social and political reality. We have discussed various schools of the sociology of literature in the last chapter, which emphasized close interaction between literature and political consciousness.

Dalit literature can not be considered as 'caste literature' rather it is political literature as Kanwal Bharati asked a very pertinent question that literature is not divided on the basis of language only (as Bengali, Kannada, Tamil, Urdu Literature and so on) but it is also divided on the basis of ideology and 'isms', for instance, *Hindutva*, Islamic, and Christian Literature; Marxist and Rightist Literature; Gandhian and Nationalist Literature and Global Literature. Then why cannot there be *Dalit* Literature, which represents voice of the majority of this country?[50]

Kanwal Bharati considers that only *Dalits* can write *Dalit* literature as they are the sufferers of multiple oppressions and they have felt trauma of caste atrocities. He regards that sympathetic upper caste authors cannot be the part of the *Dalit* literature as they won't be able to express trauma of the *Dalit* community because they have not felt it. Hence, he regards that Premchand, Nirala, Amritlal Nagar and Dr. Jagdish Gupta cannot be a part of the *Dalit* literature.[51]

The guiding force for the *Dalit* literature becomes the Ambedkarite philosophy that represents a comprehensive worldview different from the upper caste hegemonic philosophy and incorporates Buddhism, *Bhakti*sm and other protest traditions prevalent in the Indian society, like the verses of Shankaranand and Acchutanand (prevalent in Uttar Pradesh). Kanwal Bharati conclusively writes that the guiding ideology of *Dalit* authors cannot be centrist, leftist or rightist not and even *Dalitist* but can only be the Ambedkarite vision. We would discuss these issues in the subsequent chapters of this study while examining *Dalit* literature, its nature, scope and impact on the movement.

Highlighting the contribution of *Dalit* literature to the development of Indian art, culture and literature, Prof. Nandu Ram says that *Dalit* literature has immensely contributed towards the development and preservation of the Indian culture but this contribution has not been acknowledged by the historians who are upper castes, for whom the focus is limited to a particular view (upper caste hegemony) that has been projected as the representative of the Indian reality. But as a matter of fact, there are several cultural traditions, which are known by the names of *Dalit* authors and artists, *e.g.*, movements by Ravidas and Keshavnarain in U.P.; Satnami Movement in Chattisgarh; and movements by Phule in Maharashtra etc. He further elucidates that *Dalit* literature is anti-establishment and advocates a new social system based on equality, liberty and fraternity.[52] Another *Dalit* litterateur, Jai Prakash Kardam resonates the same view that the vision of the *Dalit* literature is to establish an equalitarian society that aims for the welfare of all.[53]

Thus, the *Dalit* aesthetics draws its inspiration by the Ambedkarite philosophy and the *Dalit* literature makes it a guiding force. Sharan Kumar Limbale[54] sets the following 'tests' for the formation of the *Dalit* aesthetics, *viz.*,

- Author experiences be authentic;
- Those experiences be generalized/universalized;
- Those experiences should not be just region specific; and

- Texts should instil inspiration for egalitarian social system.

He further regards that the *Dalit* aesthetics manifests expression of the cardinal values of Independence, Justice, Equality and Fraternity and the *Dalit* literature be studied with this perspective rather than considering it 'caste literature' or something that does not express in a any sophisticated form. This brings out that the *Dalit* Literature needs to represent real picture of the community, its trauma and its struggle for social change. This also recognizes the fact that literary aesthetics have been transcended from a sophisticated perspective to a realistic (sometimes may, apparently, appear harsh, rude as some of the authors argue) and true aesthetic sense that attempts to demolish the supremacy of a structured forms of literary aesthetics. It would be explored and analyse this characteristic in subsequent chapters of this study in relation to the Hindi *Dalit* Literature. We would observe that Hindi *Dalit* Literature is cultivating it own literary space with a high level of thinking which possesses the sense of freedom, essence of realistic aesthetic, constructive soul and highlight the ground realities of the *Dalit* community. Its reading and study makes us restless and leads for social change and solidarity towards the establishment of an egalitarian society.

NOTES

1. Quoted in Rebati B. Tripathy, *Dalit: A Sub-human Society* (Delhi: Ashish Publishing House, 1994) p. 2.
2. *Manifesto of the Dalit Panthers*, 1972.
3. *Ibid.*
4. Zelliot, Eleanor. *Ibid.*, p. v.
5. Ram, Nandu. *Beyond Ambedkar* (Delhi: Har-Anand Publications, 1995) p. 87.
6. Zelliot, Eleanor. *Ibid.*, p. 267.
7. Quoted in Eleanor Zelliot, *Ibid.*, p. 268.
8. *Constitution of India*, 1950.
9. Omvedt, Gail. *Dalits and Democratic Revolution: Dr. Ambedkar and the Dalit Movement in Colonial India* (Delhi:.Sage Publications, 1994) p. 11.
10. Shah, Ghanshyam. *Social Movements in India: A Review of the Literature* (Delhi: Sage Publications, 1990) p. 16.
11. For complete reference of the definition and related debates on the term, 'Movement', please see Ghanshyam Shah, *Social Movements in India* (Delhi: Sage Publications, 1990), p. 13-27. It provides a comprehensive discussion

on the subject and working definition of the term that has been adopted for this work also.

12. *Ibid.*
13. *Ibid.*
14. Morris-Jones, W.H. *The Government and Politics of India* (London: Hutchinson University Library, 1964) quoted in Ghanshyam Shah, *Ibid.*
15. Kothari, R. *'The Non-Party Political Process'* (*Economic and Political Weekly*, 19 (5), February 4, 1984) p. 218 quoted in Ghanshyam Shah, *Ibid.* p. 25.
16. Kothari, R. *'Masses, Classes and the State (Economic and Political Weekly*, 21 (5), February 1, 1986) p. 214 quoted in Ghanshyam Shah, *Ibid*, p. 25-26.
17. Wilkinson, Paul. *Social Movements* (London: Pall Mall, 1971), p. 27 quoted in Ghanshyam Shah, *Ibid.* p. 16-17.
18. Shah, Ghanshyam. *Ibid.* p. 17.
19. *Ibid.* p. 108.
20. See Eleanor Zelliot, *Ibid.* for further detail on these two saints.
21. Quoted in Eleanor Zelliot, *Ibid.* p. 5-6.
22. *Ibid.* p. 22.
23. Ranade, M.G. *Rise of Marathi Power and Other Essays* (Bombay: University of Bombay, 1961), p. 62, Quoted in Eleanor Zelliot, *Ibid.* p. 8-9.
24. In Jorden, J.T.F. *Dayanand Saraswati: His Life and Ideas* (Delhi: Oxford University Press, 1978) p. 62.
25. Shah, Ghanshyam. *Ibid.* p. 109.
26. Jurgensmeyer, M. *Religion as Social Vision: The Movement against Untouchability in 20th Century Punjab* (Berkeley: University of California Press, 1882) for detail.
27. Srinivas, M.N. *Religion and Society among Coorgs of South India* (Delhi: Oxford University Press, 1952) p. 32.
28. Quoted in Eleanor Zelliot, *Ibid.* p. 192.
29. *Ibid.* p. 218.
30. Dhasal, Namdev. In *Economic and Political Weekly*, (Volume VIII, 31-3, p. 1398) quoted in Eleanor Zelliot, *Ibid.* p. 219.
31. Webster, J.C.B. *Abstract from the First Ambedkar Chair Lecture*, 1995 (Centre for Study of Social Systems /School of Social Sciences, Jawaharlal Nehru University, Delhi).
32. Please see Joseph Benjamin. *Scheduled Cast in Indian Politics and Society* (Delhi: Ess Ess Publications, 1989) p. 26-52 for detail.
33. Omvedt, Gail. *Ibid.* p. 161.
34. Zelliot, Eleanor. *Ibid.* p. 53.
35. *Indian Statutory Commission, 16*, p. 41.
36. *Dr. Babasaheb Ambedkar: Writings and Speeches,* Vol. II, edited by Vasant Moon (Bombay: Government of Maharashtra, Education Department, 1882) p.503-6 quoted in Gail Omvedt, *Ibid.* p. 168.
37. Zelliot, Eleanor. *Ibid.* p. 166.
38. *Ibid.* p. 106.

39. *Ibid.* p. 107.
40. *The Charter of Demands* (New Delhi, Dada Sahib B.K. Gaikwad, B.P. Maurya and B.D. Khobragade for the Repuublican Party of India, 1964) quoted in Eleanor Zelliot, *Ibid.* p. 117.
41. Srinivas, M.N. *Caste in Modern India* (Bombay: Media Promoters & Publishers, 1962, reprint 1989), p. 3.
42. Dhasal, Namdev. *Ibid.*, quoted in Eleanor Zelliot, *Ibid.* p. 219.
43. Zelliot, Eleanor. *Ibid.* for further detail.
44. *Ibid.* p. v.
45. Ram, Nandu, *Ibid.* p. 31.
46. Kothari, R. *'Rise of the Dalits and the Renewed Debate on Caste' (Economic and Political Weekly*, 25 June, 1994), p. 1592.
47. Omvedt, Gail, *Ibid.* p. 326.
48. *Ibid.* p. 338.
49. Please see Tulsi Ram, *'Dalit Sahitya Ki Avdharana'* in Shyoraj Singh 'Baichan' and Devendra Choube, *Chitan Ki Parampara Aur Dalit Sahitya* (Hazaribagh: Navlakhen Prakashan, 2000-2001) p. 59-66 for detail.
50. Bharati, Kanwal (ed.) *Dalit Jan Ubhaar* (Lucknow: B.M.N. Prakshan, year not mentioned) p185 translation mine.
51. *Ibid.* translation mine.
52. Ram, Nandu. *'Bhartiya Samaj Aur Dalit'* in Shyoraj Singh 'Baichan' and Devender Chobe, *Ibid.* p. 13-21 for detail.
53. Please see *'Yudhrat Aam Aadami*' (Hazaribagh: January-June 1998) for further detail.
54. Limbale, Sharan Kumar. *Dalit Sahitya Ka Saundryashastra* (Delhi: Vani Prakashan, 2002) and also see *Yudhrat Aam Aadami* (Hazaribagh: January-June 1998) for further detail.

4

Premchand to Mannu Bhandari

Critical Analysis

The years between 1930 and 1940 were crucial years in the history of twentieth century India in general and for the *Dalit* movement, in particular. These years witnessed important developments during the National Liberation Movement *e.g.*, Civil Disobedience (1930-31), Gandhi-Irwin Pact (March 5, 1931), Second Round Table Conference, Communal Award (August 1932), Government of India Act, 1935 and twenty-eight months of the Congress Rule, peasants uprisings and more intensive attack on the British *Raj*.

The *Dalit* Movement in India experienced crucial developments during this phase as recorded by Gail Omvedt that "these years saw the All-India Depressed Classes Conference at Nagpur in 1930; Ambedkar's attendance at the First Round Table Conference; his clash with Gandhi before and at the Second Round Table Conference, culminating in the Poona Pact of 1932; and the famous conversion announcement in 1935, 'I have been born a Hindu but I will not die a Hindu". She further noted "the events of 1930-32 led to Ambedkar's final disillusionment with Hinduism, with even the best and most 'reformist' of the Congress leadership. At the same time these events revealed the power represented by Ambedkar and by the *Dalit* movement which had risen with him and confirmed his as the unparalleled leader of the *Dalits*, forcing the Congress leadership to deal with his demands."[1] This was the same period when northern India was also experiencing *Dalit* uprisings as we have already discussed in the last chapter that level of political consciousness among *Dalits* got enhanced with its political articulation and expression. All these developments, particularly Ambedkar's leadership was immensely influencing the very shape and expression of political consciousness among *Dalits*.

It is important to note that during these years, the *Dalit* movement was attempting to explore the possibilities for autonomy, identity, mobilisation and empowerment under the dynamic leadership of Dr. Ambedkar. *Dalit* movement was shaping itself not on the lines of the 'Reformative movements' but attempting to create an alternative socio-cultural structure for an egalitarian society.

In northern India, we find that there was political assertion during mid-1920s up to 1930 by the *Dalits* in the forms of the *Adi Hindu* Ideology, *Bhakti* Resurgence and challenge to the Arya Samaj's *Shuddhi* campaign. Recent research on the *Dalit* movement highlights various levels of assertion during these years. For instance, leaders like Swami Acchutanand (1879-1933) and Ram Charan (1888-1938) were highlighting importance of education, economic independence, social and religious reforms and asserting a dignified self-identity which is inherently political with equal status.[2] Swami Acchutanand organised a massive 'Untouchable Conference' in 1922 at Old Fort, Delhi and proposed a 17-point Charter of Demands to the Prince of Wales that primarily asked for the political representation of the *Dalits* in all the local and provincial bodies. Responding to the Charter of Demands, the then Secretary of State ordered nomination of at least one representative from the *Dalit* community to the local bodies. It also ordered all district authorities that Swami Acchutanand be given permission to organise conferences and rallies wherever he wishes. This was a significant achievement and Swamiji subsequently organised several rallies and conference in different parts of Uttar Pradesh and attended such events in other provinces of the country for the cause of *Dalit* upliftment. He used to start his address with the following lines, which itself reflect his political understanding:

> "Sabhya Sabse Hind Ke Pracheen Hakdaar Hum;
> Tha Banaya Shudra Humko, Theya kabhi Sardar Hum;
> Ab Nahin Hai Voh Zamana, Zulum Harihar Mat Saho;
> Tod do Zanjeer, Jakede Kyon Gulaami Mein raho."[3]

This roughly means that we were the most ancient people of India, who had all rights; we were made *'Shudra'* while we used to be the kings; now that time has gone, do not tolerate oppression; break chains, why to remain slaves?

Significantly, Ambedkar's influence was spreading in the northern India and people from the *Dalit* community were making a conscious attempts to challenge *Brahmanical* Caste System at all possible levels: intellectually, politically and socially, with explorations from the historical anecdotes like popularising Ravidas and Kabir; establishing contacts with the Marathi *Dalit* Literature; proliferating ideas of Phule and Dr. Ambedkar and participating in the Freedom Struggle with a vision of Independent India where equality, liberty and fraternity could be ensured to all. Here it is important to recall that Dr. Ambedkar was leading the *Dalit* movement with an untiring zeal making it broad based and mobilising community at an all-India level. He was instrumental in all political and social initiatives, contributed to the formation of three political parties and launching conversion movement challenging the very foundation of the Caste System. We have already discussed his role in the *Dalit* movement in the last chapter.

Thus, the years between 1930 and 1940 were crucial in the history of the *Dalit* movement in India and developments during these years had positive impact on the course of the movement. An all-round challenge to the *Brahmanical* social norms and caste system was being felt in all walks of life and we find that Hindi literature was also responding to these issues and Premchand became the prominent figure to address these issue in his works.

Premchand (1880-1936) was writing during the first half of the twentieth century when India was facing colonialism, imperialism and National Liberation Movement. He wrote on a variety of subjects touching almost each and every aspect of the contemporary Indian social and political life. Right from the beginning of his creative life, he advocated the cause of peasantry, exploited and deprived sections of society. He understood that writers have a mission to envisage revolutionary changes and must perform a committed role "in nurturing the literary and artistic trend which brings awakening and freshness in society and throw light on real problems of the people."[4] He resigned from his government job in 1921 after attending a public meeting addressed by Gandhiji who appealed people to join non-cooperation movement and contributed to the Freedom Struggle as a writer-activist. His ranging writings are voluminous from novels, plays, short stories, essays and journalistic write-ups with extensive notes on contemporary subjects that reshaped the very course (including the content and form) of the Hindi literature, which got immensely influenced by his style and narrative.

Literature, for Premchand, becomes the beacon for politics that guides; it is "exploration for harmony"[5] having equality, liberty, solidarity, compassion and independence as the cardinal principles to cherish with "idealistic realism"[6] that "generates dynamism, struggle and uneasiness"[7] and a new aesthetic sense has to be evolved that testifies "a sense of independence, essence of aesthetics, soul of reconstruction and regeneration embedded in the problems of life."[8]

It is this understanding of literature that led Premchand to write on different contemporary issues, which were being faced by his times. He also wrote on the problems of Untouchability along with other subjects in his journalistic write-ups, novels and short stories. Initially, he wrote with the Gandhian perspective but subsequently, got influenced by Dr. Ambedkar. In his later writings, we find that Premchand considered that the problem of Untouchability cannot be resolved unless the inherently exploitative Caste System is liquidated and *Dalits* are economically empowered and made politically assertive. He regarded Dr. Ambedkar as an unparalleled leader of the community and got inspiration from the on-going *Dalit* movement that Dr. Ambedkar was leading during the first half of the last century.

Now, we would discuss some of the writings of Premchand that are either directly on the *Dalits* characters or have implications to that effect. This is being done in two ways: first, we would discuss some of his stories in a general way and then his story *Kafan* and novel *Godan* in detail to have a comprehensive analysis of his understanding of the issues.

Here it is important to note that Premchand was having a wide meaning of the term 'untouchable castes' that include both the 'Scheduled Castes' and the 'Other Backward Castes'. The term *Dalit* is not very often used in his literature and if at all it has been used, it does not connote the political meaning that the term had acquired. Instead, Premchand used to mention the particular castes of the characters and also narrated prevalent views (which represented largely upper castes views) on those castes, for instance, in his stories like '*Thakur Ka Kuan*', '*Mukti Marg*' etc. There are overlapping usages of the deprived, lower and other backward castes in his literature. In some of his stories, castes of the lead characters have not been mentioned but the descriptive narrative provides several inferences to their caste status. Moreover, the context of his stories and novels is largely rural and he tried to reflect rural life in the country, attempting to present it in holistic manner. *Muktimarg, Mantra, Poos Ki Raat, Algoajha, Kajaki, Sadgati, Mandir, Dhoodh Ka Daam, Gulli Danda,* and *Kafan* are some of his short stories, which focus on different aspects of the problems of the *Dalit* community.

In all his stories he related to the problems of 'Untouchability'. Premchand made an attempt to highlight the level of exploitation, which is inherent in the Caste System, and described traumatic and painful life through which the *Dalit* community was undergoing during these periods. At the same time, he exposed the hypocrisy of the upper castes and how they were trying to maintain their hegemony to sustain the oppressive caste system. Though he was influenced by the contemporary *Dalit* movement, led by Dr. Ambedkar, but in most of his stories, his style is descriptive rather than prescriptive whereas in his other works. he has either presented 'Gandhian vision of transformation of hearts' or some socialistic kind of vision for social change. This may be understood by the prevalent political scenario in the northern India where the *Dalit* movement was, apparently, not articulate and the over-all political fabric was guided by the Freedom Struggle led by Gandhiji. But there is a peculiar characteristic in all his writings that he always attacked the hypocrisy that was maintained by the upper castes and to expose the limitless exploitation of the *Dalits*.

At the same time, Premchand apparently, was, influenced by the contemporary *Dalit* movement when he was writing stories like *Mandir* and *Mantra* where issue like temple entry and *'Shuddhi'* were addressed. *Thakur Ka Kaun* was centred on the issue of drinking water and the problem of 'Untouchability'. There are stories, which are directly written on the *Dalit* issues, on the level of social and economic exploitation, temple entry, social disabilities imposed on the *Dalits*, common community feast and the hypocrisy of the upper castes. Premchand has highlighted the level of economic and social exploitation being faced by the *Dalits* and simultaneously he also emphasised on the humane qualities possessed by the *Dalits vis-à-vis* upper castes. He directly attacked the '*Varna* System' and social hierarchy and envisioned a strong challenge to break these oppressive systems.

Though Premchand has not written any particular novel directly on the *Dalit* issue (except *Karmbhoomi* partially) we find that there are several references (direct or indirect, whether inter-caste marriages, *Begar*, economic exploitation, social disabilities or land rights issues) to the problems in many of his novels. In *Godan* also, the central character is not a *Dalit* but apparently belongs to the 'Other Backward Caste' but, as mentioned earlier, there has been overlapping usages of the castes in Premchand's writings. Now we would discuss two specific works by Premchand: Kafan and *Godan*.

Kafan (1936, Story): Premchand

The story Kafan (The Shroud) was written in 1936, the year Premchand died and is the most famous as well as a controversial story. The story narrates the life of a *Dalit* family (Ghisu and, his son, Madhav and daughter-in-law, Budhia) who are devastated by poverty. The whole plot is embedded in the rural society where this family is the poorest one. The story starts with conversation between father and son about his daughter-in-law who is pregnant and facing labour pain. Both, Ghisu and Madhav are presented as notoriously lazy who do not want to do any work at all, fearing nothing and "living at a sub-human level they are outside all normal mores of social behaviour. While Madhav's wife is writhing in labour pain inside the hut, Madhav and his father sit outside, greedily devouring stolen potatoes, unwilling to go and help her because the other person might grab a larger share. Ghisu recounts in detail a feast to which he had been invited twenty years ago and Madhav listens to the vivid account of food with vicarious pleasure. The wife lies dying inside"[9] and both of them slept unconcerned about her.

Next morning, Budhia is dead. Both, father and son started mourning. The neighbours came and expressed their condolences. Now arrangements for the cremation are to be made. There was nothing in the house and both of them had no money at all. They went to the *Zamindar* who gave them two rupees with contempt. Other people from the village also donated some money for cremation. They now collected some five rupees and went to purchase the shroud. They looked for a cheap shroud but failed and entered into a tavern where they drank and ate forgetting all their responsibilities and fearing nothing. While drinking, they commented on several things including rituals, traditions and system and praised Budhia "who even in death provided them food and drink."[10] They got heavily intoxicated and in the end, started singing, dancing and wiggling just to fell down unconscious. The story comes to an end.

This is Premchand's most controversial story that invited numerous interpretations by critics. Meenakshi Mukherjee considers this story "almost perfect distillation of a situation that disturbs the reader with intense but understated horror."[11] She further elaborates that "in reading Kafan one remembers Engels' advice to Margaret Harkness: 'The more the opinion of the author remain hidden, the better for the work of art'. The radical questions that are raised in the story do not have very simple answers."[12] It is important to note that this story is completely descriptive and analytical rather than prescriptive and ideal. It does not provide any "solution of a question"[13] but contextualised "the correct setting of a question"[14] which is "obligatory for an artist."[15] Kafan becomes "most memorable of Premchand's stories because, although nothing is solved here, the question has been stated precisely and disconcertingly. In a society where even hard work and honest labour do not raise a man's life very much above the animal level, how does one condemn Ghisu's and his son's rebellion? 'What kind of custom is it when a living person does not get a rag to cover his body, the dead must have a new shroud?' asks Ghisu. But even when one rationalizes the that the mourning is a luxury a starving man cannot afford, it is difficult to condone the action of Madhav and Ghisu. At the same time it is not easy to take the side of a society that reluctantly proffers a few coins for the dead, more to keep up a pretence than out of any real concern for the human beings. The story disturbs because one sees the precariousness of our cherished human values, with bestiality on one side and hypocrisy on the other. The concentrated horror of the story arises out of the reader's inability to take sides. Since Premchand's style is totally devoid of poetry and resonance, his optimum effect can be achieved in the direction of starkness, and nowhere is this better illustrated than in Kafan."[16]

Bhisma Sahni finds the story "striking a note of deep anguish and tragedy."[17] Analysing Premchand's style as a short story writer,

Sahni further points out "the poorest of the poor are shown in the extremity of their condition, beyond which there are only terrors awaiting them. The stark simplicity of these stories presents their condition in all nakedness. They require no comment, no sermonizing, no rhetorical embellishments. They speak for themselves. And they are the products not so much of the anger and resentment that the author feels about the human situation, but of deep anguish."[18] Surendra Chowdhry regards the structure of the story as "macrocosmic that has two major characteristics: first, a lively and eventful illustration of rural life and second, state of merciless economic exploitation prevalent in the society...the story is both realistic as well as symbolic and raises several questions about the contemporary socio-cultural and economic systems."[19] Many other critics regard Kafan as a story representing "psychological realism"[20] that has been conceptualised in a realistic background highlighting the level of economic exploitation and how lack of money "dehumanises."[21] Kafan, in fact, represents two disequilibriums that are not identical and also "defamiliarised of reality"[22] where reader "is not experiencing reality but understanding its complex mechanics. Things like that do not happen in life, but they must happen in literature to make life more intelligible. Here the given system of relationship is not saved but exposed to insecurity-rendered vulnerable. Here everything is so disclosed that we may like to change it."[23]

There has been a new wave of interpretations of Premchand's work and, particularly of this story, especially by the *Dalit* litterateurs. Before we dwell upon some of the recent interpretations, it is to be noted that these interpretations are taking place amidst an atmosphere characterised by the contemporary political vision that attempts to define and redefine (and sometime, evaluates and re-evaluates) the past, its histories and cultures. This also applies to literature and thus, new interpretations of the works, either done by the *Dalit* or non-*Dalit* writers are coming. This is also influenced by the fact where *Dalit* writers consider that literature cannot be devoid of the on-going *Dalit* movement and it is an effective instrument to broaden and consolidate the movement further. Hence, it needs to be analysed politically, consistent with the vision of the *Dalit* movement. Another important factor to be reiterated is the debate over the issue of literature written by *Dalits* or for *Dalits* by upper castes. This is, in a way, sympathy and empathy factor and we have already discussed it in the last chapter. *Dalit* litterateurs feel that the *Dalit* movement and its assertion, especially through literature, has to be free from all kinds of *Brahamanical* influences and must have an autonomous character led by *Dalits* themselves. It is this understanding of the contemporary *Dalit* movement and *Dalit* literature that has led to the re-interpretations of several literary works including Premchand's.

This new wave of re-interpretation starts from the renowned *Dalit* litterateur, Om Prakash Balmiki who, in his Presidential Address to the Conference of Hindi *Dalit* Writers in Nagpur (October 21-22,1993), made a comment on Premchand's short stories and their paradox, where he said, "Premchand has written several important stories on *Dalit* consciousness like *Sadgati, Thakur Ka Kuan, Dhoodh Ka Daam* etc. but coming to his last phase story *Kafan*, he seems to be an advocate of Gandhian principles, feudal values and *'Varna'* system. There is a paradox in his works-one, sympathy with the *Dalits* and other belief in the *'Varna'* System."[24] This led to a series of articles and journalistic write-ups by both the *Dalits* and non-*Dalits* on Premchand, his literary works (both novels and short stories) and his political vision of *Dalit* liberation.

Here, it is important to note that the Dalit writers have made this effort themselves who questioned the very message of Premchand's writings and hence, his political vision. Most of them found Kafan "an undoubtedly anti-*Dalit* story,"[25] as pointed out by Kanwal Bharati, "though it should not be concluded from this story that Premchand was not sympathetic with the *Dalits* but this fact also cannot be repudiated that he ridiculed the life of *Dalits* in this story."[26] Several *Dalit* writers have emphasised Gandhian influence on Premchand's writings and political understanding, which is largely correct as has been manifested in most of his literary works. But, as mentioned earlier the political fabric in Uttar Pradesh during 1930s was the influenced (largely dominated) by the Gandhian rather than the Ambedkarite discourse, though there were representatives like Swami Acchutanand and others who were propagating Ambedkarite vision for *Dalit* liberation. This definitely had an impact on Premchand's writings and Gandhiji immensely influenced him as is evident from his resignation on Gandhi's appeal, his numerous write-ups on Gandhi and his politics and other references made in different journals. This also shaped his political understanding that got manifested in his literary works where he, in most of his works, prescribed 'transformation of hearts' especially in the context of the upper and lower castes, making 'Untouchability' a 'moral' issue.

Some other *Dalit* writers like Shyoraj Singh 'Bechain' consider that Kafan is far from realism and "completely an imaginative story to prove that *Dalits* are not humane...and the purpose of this story is to portray a totally distorted picture of the *Dalit* community."[27] Kanwal Bharati, in another article, reiterates, "Kafan is an anti-*Dalit* story because it has made a mockery of the *Dalits* through its characters who have been portrayed insensitive and inhumane."[28] Here it needs to be pointed out that both Om Prakash Balmiki and Kanwal Bharti have appreciated Premchand's works and his concerns for the *Dalit* cause. Kanwal Bharati made it clear when he says, "it is not doubtful that Premchand was the first person, among the upper castes, who voiced the *Dalit* cause. He was against Untouchability and made efforts to eliminate it. But, despite this fact, *Dalits* cannot consider his literature as the *Dalit* literature. It was written out of sympathy and several national and international pressures can also not be ignored for its creation."[29] He further emphasised that "it would be wrong to conclude that we are against Premchand. We are neither against Premchand nor Premchand was against the *Dalits*. His stories on the *Dalits* and their lives were based on his understanding of the contemporary *Dalit* discourse. We may agree or disagree with him today but *Dalit* discourse and its exponents have every right to reinterpret and re-evaluate Premchand and these interpretations should be understood as the statement of this right by the *Dalit* writers."[30] Thus, it can be concluded that Kafan in isolation represents a work produced by the insensitive and exploitative socio-economic system that leads to dehumanisation but at the same time it cannot be understood as a story representing the *Dalit* community, as has been discussed above.

Godan (1936, Novel): Premchand

Premchand is known for realistic novels and has been regarded by many critics as the Emperor of Hindi novels. He was writing within a "historical context that was dominated by feudal system and its values, colonialism, slavery and exploitation and also with the growing capitalistic system... Premchand's creativity is contextualised by the National Freedom Struggle, which focussed itself against British Colonialism, Capitalism and Feudalism. This context has a very important effect on his writings and we find that those are essentially anti-feudal, anti-capitalist and anti-colonial."[31] Gandhian and socialistic philosophy, as we have already seen, influenced his political vision and "essentially he was a humanist...his humanism was firmly rooted in material life and was basically practical...governed by moral values, by the concepts of the good and the evil, the right and the wrong."[32] This "essential humanism" is all pervasive in his writings, especially novels. He is not a realist in technically strict European sense but he is a realist with a vision, with a mission and with "author's own intensive experience of social process"[33] who portray human life with all its charm, excitement, love, affection, faith, morals, tension, pain, trauma, misery, pessimism and optimism.

Most of his novels have been written with peasants as the lead characters and with villages as the centre stage. This is a very peculiar feature of his novels and makes his task much difficult to portray a realistic view. "But this is the evidence of Premchand's creative excellence and his thorough understanding of the peasantry and their life that led him to write on the peasants with artistic portrayal of their lives, its realities and expectations. This effort also laid the foundation for realistic tradition of the Indian novel."[34] This effort also "widened the frontiers of realism so as to include in its orbit the peasant and the rural masses, most effectively. The village for Premchand was not an idyllic paradise but a world full of tension, conflict and struggle. The centre of the stage which was till then reserved only for the middle class visionary was for the first time thrown open to the village yoke, who was representing the contemporary situation much more effectively than any other segment of Indian society. And, he could do it with the help of real characters from the countryside, drawing richly his own experience, which gives validity and authenticity to his art...he was the first from novelist to reach the rural society. He was, again, the first artist to view and present our rural society not as an idyll but as an arena of life built of conflicting power groups. His village is, in fact, the picture of mini-India with all its contradiction, pulls and pressures, aspirations and failures, power and potentials. It is this complex but live reality which lends colour, beauty, power and sublimity to his art."[35]

There is a holistic representation in the portrayal of life, with its totality, of his characters, with artistic unity highlighting on the rural and urban settings, dialectical and contradictory association of individuals with the socio-eco-cultural systems and a vision to achieve harmony. He wrote novels on a variety of subjects dealing with Freedom Struggle, capitalism, feudalism and colonialism, 'Untouchability' widow re-marriage and prostitution. There is no direct novel on 'Untouchability' (except *Karambhoomi*) but there are several reflections in almost every novel on this issue. This may be said here that the 'Untouchability' was the social reality of his times and as a realistic, he couldn't afford to ignore it while depicting a realistic picture of the Indian society. The way this problem has been depicted, it can be analysed with two perspectives: one, politically, it is guided by the Gandhian approach and two, artistically, it has presented a very realistic depiction of the community, their trauma and pain and in doing so Premchand also expressed his understanding of the issue, which, sometimes but in a limited ways, goes beyond the Gandhian approach. This transcendence of thought is characteristically important to analyse the works of Premchand because "as a writer with a social role and responsibility"[36] Premchand was having a political vision, close to Gandhi, but as literary aesthetician, he transcends his political worldview that becomes 'essentially humanist'. With this understanding of his political and literary vision, we would now analyse his most celebrated work *Godan*.

Godan was published in 1936, some months before Premchand's death, and got world wide acclaim, established a new tradition of Indian novel writings and above all presented a very authentic and realistic view of the contemporary Indian peasants and middle class lives. Many critics consider it "as a saga of Indian rural life whose protagonist Hori is the archetypal Indian peasant in his meekness and humanity."[37] The plot is, apparently, very simple that narrates the life and the struggle for life of its protagonist, Hori along with his family (Dhania, his wife, Gobar, his son, Sona and Rupa, his daughters and his brothers) who live in a village called *Belari*, somewhere in the *Awadh* province, in acute poverty and struggles everyday either in the field or elsewhere to earn a square meal a day, which becomes the toughest task throughout their lives. The family (especially Hori) is trapped in the worst network of vicious circle of poverty, debt and ritual conservatism that was characteristic of the Indian peasants' life during the first half of the last century.

The novel depicts, in the best tradition of literary expression, hopes and despairs, optimism and pessimism and rebellion analysing the very mindset of the farmers, *zamindars*, moneylenders, priests and others in the villages of India and exploitation of the poor at all levels comes out as the central concern of the novel. The novel also narrates the dynamics of the village life, particularly the inter-community dynamics, and its politics. This has been done in a holistic manner (not emphasising on any one particular community or system) keeping, objectively, the life of the peasants and their exploitation in the centre of the novel, highlighting problems of debt, 'Untouchability', '*Varna* system', *zamindari* system, *'Begar'* and over-all political system of the pre-Independence Indian society.

The objective holistic construction of the novel would be evident from a very quick look on the major characters, which represents almost the whole gamut of the contemporary Indian society. For instance, Hori has been described as the representative of the Indian peasant who "is the victim of social determinism"[38] but humane and honest, with land as his cherished value and cow a life-long dream. Dhania, "a sharp-tongued yet tender, compassionate and querulous by turns, in open rebellion against her oppressors yet traditional in certain basic way"[39] represents best model of traditional and illiterate rural womenfolk. Gobar is a growing youth representing anger and fear; ambition and cowardice. Datadin epitomises priestly Brahman class in the village and Silia represents the *Dalit* community.

"Rai Saheb (*Zamindar*) is another character who oscillates between two modes. He depends almost entirely on his estate for survival and is not above squeezing his poor tenants when he needs money, yet the author is eager to show that he is really not a crook at all-perhaps merely a victim of circumstance."[40] Mehta represents intelligentsia while Malti does for the western educated urban Indian woman; Khanna embodies values of the industrial capitalism. It is precisely due to this holistic construction of the novel that *Godan* has been regarded 'the prose epic' by many critics.

The plot is interwoven with the urban life representing the urban middle class (Mehta, Malti, Khanna, Onkar Nath and others in their circle) and its contradictions (particularly in terms of tradition-modernity dichotomy) that raises several questions faced by the contemporary middle class breeding disappointment, isolation and rootlessness. At the story level, these strands: urban and rural "are interlinked through contrasts and parallels, but in the 'discourse' the gap between them presents an aesthetic problem."[41] Some other critics like Meenakshi Mukherjee find more than two strands at the story level[42] which are important in the analysis of the novel, *viz.*,

(*a*) Hori's story, and around him the story of his family and his village;
(*b*) Gobar's story, moving from the village to the city;
(*c*) Rai Saheb's story, straddling the village and the city; and
(*d*) Mehta and Malti's story, and that of their coterie in the city.

Here it is noticeable that how each of the above four strands are well connected as has been emphasised by Meenakshi Mukherjee that "A and B begin together although B branches off later; C and D are closely connected because although Rai Saheb's land is in the village he has social as well as financial dealings with the urban professional class. Premchand takes care to interlink the different strands in as many ways as possible. A and B touch because there is a feudal relationship between Rai Saheb and Hori; B and D are connected because Gobar is first employed by Mirza Khursheed in the city, later by Dr. Malti Kaul. A and D get linked when Mehta and Malti come to the village to help the people of Belari. Only B and C never meet or converge."[43]

Thus, *Godan* becomes a classic novel on the Indian peasantry and is objectively well knit and carefully interwoven. But if we take into account the whole range of works by Premchand, we find that *Godan* also represents his disillusionment with the system and from the prescriptive narrative, as unlike his other works including short stories, he does not suggest any solution. "*Godan* has no utopia to look forward to or fall back on. Since there is no system to be saved, the novel begins with a disequilibrium and ends at a disequilibrium. It excites a sense of profound wrong done to humanity. It makes no attempt at papering the cracks or providing a happy ending. In fact, such a piece of literary art goes beyond the text and establishes a living relationship with life. It is literature of this type, that, according to Sartre, succeeds through failure…"[44]

Coming to the political consciousness among the *Dalits* as represented in the *Godan*, we find that there is only representational depiction of the issue but this representational narrative is, unlike any other work of Premchand, powerful one. As we have mentioned earlier there are overlapping usages of different castes in Premchand's literature, in this novel also, the caste of the protagonist, Hori is not mentioned though there are some indicators to infer his caste identity. For example, there is a reference to his caste status when Datadeen trapped him for sharing his crop and deceivingly said, "I'm not your foe. You annoy me. My good man, what was there to feel so delicate about? We are all in it together, aren't we? How does it matter if you are a low caste (*'Shudra'* in Hindi version) and I am *Brahmin*? We are all members of one family. Oh, we all have our ups and downs. If something happens to me tomorrow, whose help will I seek if not yours?"[45] This reference, along with some other ones, indicates that Hori belongs to the lower caste and represents them, who are poor, debt-trapped and exploited.

If we explore his political mind, we find that he was also representing the contemporary political understanding prevalent in his community that was exploited in the name of religion, tradition or prestige. It is to be noted that the protagonist is also illiterate, inarticulate, fatalistic and poor. At the same time, his son, Gobar is representing the young generation, though rebellion (in its embryonic form) but also not articulated politically, who refuses to be 'a victim of circumstances' but in the end fall prey to these circumstances, despite his efforts to change the life of his family and himself. It should be kept in mind here that the whole novel is contextualised in the northern Indian village, where there was no political leader like Ambedkar and the voice of the *Dalit* community was not expressed politically.

But there is another reference in *Godan* that addresses *Dalit* discourse in significant ways. This is the Matadeen and Selia episode. Matadeen is the son of the village priest, Datadeen and Selia is a *Dalit* (*'Chamar'* in Hindi version) woman. She loves Matadeen and has also got physical association with him but Datadeen maintains, despite physical intimacy and her devotion, a distance with her due to her caste status and treats her with disrespect and indignity as Premchand mentions that Matadeen "cunningly exploited her love for him: now she was no more than a machine which worked at his bidding."[46] Matadeen also humiliated her when she was giving handful of grain as return of her debt to Dulari from his stock, which was practically the result of her labour. Further, when she asked from Matadeen, "Have I no right over your things?' Matadeen, shamelessly replied, "no, "you have no claim over me. You work, you are paid for it. If you want to give away my things, you can't do it. If this work does not suit you, find another. There is no shortage of workers here."[47] (This is English translation and does not convey proper meaning of the Hindi version, which is very harsh and blunt. Last line of Matadeen's speech is also not translated that says, "this is not *Begar*; we are giving food and clothes for this."). Selia felt deeply hurt and humiliated.

This indicates the oppressive and humiliating treatment by the upper castes for *Dalits*. They exploited *Dalits* in all possible ways: socially, economically and physically. Here Premchand has portrayed Selia's pain in a serious and delicate manner when he writes, "Selia looked helplessly at Matadeen like a bird which has been turned out of the cage with wings clipped."[48] "It was difficult to say whether she was feeling pain much or condemning...she said nothing. She resumed work with broken heart and inactive hands experiencing a lump of salt in her throat."[49] This episode, till this point of time in the novel, points out the helplessness of the *Dalit* women, who were not finding political ways to articulate their anger and were made feeble even to protest. But immediately after this incident, another incident took place, which is very political in its expression and represents another discourse of the *Dalit* movement during those times.

A group of *Dalit* community led by Selia's father, mother, two brothers, surrounded Matadeen and subsequently snapped his sacred thread (*'janayu'*) and forced him to eat a piece of bone as a mark of protest and 'revenge' for his deeds. Her father, Harkhu said, "we shall degrade Matadeen to a cobbler's (*'Chamar'* in Hindi version) position, even if we have to shed our blood to do so. Selia is a girl; she has to live with one man or the other. We have no quarrel on this point. But whoever keeps her must keep her with dignity. If you can't make us Brahmins, we can make you cobblers."[50] "If you can make us Brahmins, make us, our whole community is ready and if you don't have that guts, then you also be '*Chamars'*. Live with us and eat with us."[51] Afterwards, "two cobblers dashed forward and seized Matadeen's hands. The third pulled and snapped his sacred thread. Before Datadeen and Jhenguri Singh could recover from their surprise, two cobblers had thrust a big piece of bone into Matadeen's mouth. Matadeen clenched his teeth but even then the loathsome object got between his lips. His gorge rose and as his lips opened the bone slipped into his mouth. Attracted by the noise, people came running. Strangely enough no one came forward to grapple with the defilers of *dharma*, Matadeen had alienated on and all by his objectionable behaviour with the young girls of the village. Outwardly the villagers put up a show of fight; at heart they were pleased to see Matadeen getting a taste of his own medicine."[52]

Premchand narrates this incident in a delicate way and comments on hypocrisy of Brahaminism when he writes, "Matadeen stretched himself on the ground. He felt listless. His Brahmin's vanity had vanished into thin air. That piece of bone had not only polluted his mouth but his soul also. However much penance he might do, however much holy water he drank, however much money he gave in charity, however many pilgrimages he undertook, his lost *dharma* would not return. From today he would be considered an untouchable in his own house."[53] Towards the end of this incident, we find that Selia was given shelter by Dhania, who justified her father and community's action. Dhania supported their action saying, "All men are alike. When Matadeen humiliated Selia, no one raised a litter finger in protest, but when Matadeen comes in for trouble, he gets all the sympathy in the world. Has Selia no *dharma* of her own? That man Harkhu did well in beating up these holy *goondas*..."[54]

Now Selia is living in Hori's house and has one son, Ramu who is very naughty. Matadeen was 'purified' through *'shuddhi yagna'* by the Pundits of *Benaras*. But this 'purification' has changed him a lot as Premchand writes, "well, the penance did really purify him: from that day he developed a revulsion for *dharma*, discarded the sacred thread, and dumped his priesthood in the Ganga. For he realised that although his patron still asked him to work out auspicious dates and consulted him in matters of marriages and births, they refused water from his hands and did not allow him to touch their utensils: this in spite of the fact that the Pundits of Benaras had accepted him as a Brahmin. In disgust, he turned a tiller of the soil."[55] He has realised that his religion is hypocritcal and has double standards. Now he, somehow, tries to be with Selia, especially her son. One day, her son Ramu dies due to pneumonia and this becomes a critical juncture in the life of Matadeen, who now comes openly in grief and "carried the dead body (of Ramu) to the cremation ground by the side of the river, a mile away. For eight days 'his hands remained stiff. He is not ashamed today, has no hesitation."[56] After one month of Ramu's death, he came to Selia and dedicated himself to her, fully repented and changed. Here also, the whole narrative used by Premchand is noteworthy. For instance, when he comes to Selia saying, "I am not afraid of anyone"[57] and then moves towards Selia's house and declared to be there, "this is our house, this is my temple."[58] And when Selia asked, "how will you remain a Brahmin?" he replied boldly, "I want to be a cobbler (*Chamar* in Hindi version). All those who fulfil their *dharma* are Brahmins, all those who violate their *dharma* are cobblers."[59] And in this way, he becomes fully devoted to Selia demolishing false *Brahmanism*, which he realised was a sham.

There have been numerous interpretations of the Matadeen-Selia episode by the critics. Some found it progressive keeping in mind the time and space of the novel. Sadanand Shahi regards that this incident "exposed not only the very hypocrisy of the '*Varna* system' but also advocates *Dalits*' protest to this. This prepares a background for the future *Dalit* movement that has dignity and equality as its primary goals."[60] Some other critics argued that Ambedkar rather than Gandhi *vis-à-vis* this incident influences Premchand and he would have been affected by the Temple Entry and other radical movements led by Dr. Ambedkar in the western part of the country.

Several *Dalit* critics like Kanwal Bharati and Shyoraj Singh 'Bechain' have also interpreted this episode in different ways. They regard that though Premchand depicted problems of the *Dalit* community but in the final analysis the question remains as to who got liberated: Matadeen or Selia? In the end, Matadeen transformed himself and became *'Chamar'* but the Brahmins and other upper castes did not accept Selia. This, in their opinion, is another contradiction in Premchand's writing, where there may be some instance (in fact, this episode is the one of the very few instances) of individual transformation but the upper castes, in general, have not accepted the lower castes. In fact, this reflects the contemporary *Dalit* discourse that was prevalent in northern India where, different kinds of activities like *'Shuddhi'* and others were taking place to consolidate their position as highlighted by Swami Achhutanand, as discussed earlier. But these paradoxes are to be analysed contextually along with other paradoxes (for example, characterisation of Rai Saheb, Mehta and Malti) and these are examples of "coexistence of contradictory traits"[61] and "the paradoxes inherent in *Godan*, though not always creative or fruitful, have to be seen in terms of the peculiar tensions of Premchand's time, both in his life and in Indian literary history."[62]

It is evident by now that Premchand's literature deals with variety of issues including oppression of the *Dalit* community, which remained an unavoidable social reality of his times. Before moving to analyse another work of Hindi literature on the life of the *Dalits*, Dharti Dhan Na Apana (1972) by Jagdish Chandra, it would be pertinent to have a quick understanding of the politics during the intervening period.

The focus of the *Dalit* movement during 1930 to 1950 was on the struggle for recognition of human existence and socio-political right. It was during these years that some parts of the United Province got inspired by the Ambedkarite approach to *Dalit* liberation and started addressing this issue politically. We have seen, earlier in this work, that Swami Achuutanand and Baba Ram Charan, who got inspired by Dr. Ambedkar, were leading the *Dalit* community in their struggle. Differences between Ambedkar and Gandhi were having impact shaping *Dalit* identity in this part, though with a slow and gradual development of the *Dalit* consciousness. It has also been discussed that the Gandhian framework largely influenced northern India but by mid-1940s a section of *Dalits* (disillusioned from the Arya Samaj and Reformist movements) rejected his framework and moved towards adopting the ideas of Dr. Ambedkar.

We find that Jatavas in Agra formed the *Jatava* Youth League, which by 1941, had branches in Rajasthan, Punjab and Madhya Bharat. In 1944 another important development, the formation of United

Province Scheduled Castes Federation, took place, which was formed under the influence of Dr. Ambedkar's All-India Scheduled Castes Federation. All these developments were preparing the ground for consolidated political mobilisation, which subsequently led to the formation of the Republican Party of India (RPI) in 1956. Conversion to Buddhism, led by Dr. Ambedkar in 1956, had a great ripple effect that "freed the Scheduled Castes from mental and psychological enslavement"[63] heralding a new era in the course of the *Dalit* movement making the issues of identity, mobilisation and empowerment the very focus of the struggle. During 1960s, two other important factors affected the identity formation among the *Dalits*, *viz.*, the temporary decline of the Indian National Congress after the 1967 elections and entry of the middle and backwards classes (OBCs) into politics that reflected changing caste composition in the region. Though RPI had a brief political existence (due to its internal factions, lack of dynamic leadership and appropriation by the Congress), it had great impact on the process of identity formation among *Dalits*. During early 1970s, "the most interesting socio-political development among Ambedkar's followers is the rise of the *Dalit* Panthers, a militant group of young educated Buddhists...(who) offered a challenge to unite to the politicians in Ambedkar's movement and attempted to counter violence against Untouchables in the village."[64] The *Dalit* Panthers also brought to the fore emerging *Dalit* literature (especially in Marathi) and immensely contributed for a "tough, realistic, unorthodox literature, (and) a new socio-political movement."[65]

All these developments had a gradual but great impact on formation of the *Dalit* identity and their political consciousness, though there were significant variations in its expression at the all-India level as has been noticed by Sudha Pai, "the pace of change was however, different in different regions leading to uneven development of the *Dalit* movement across the subcontinent in the post-Independence period. While parts of colonial Southern and Western India experienced strong movements demanding reservations and improved social status under leaders such as B.R. Ambedkar and M.C. Rajah, these were conspicuous by their absence in most parts of north India. In U.P., the lack of an anti-caste ideology or social reform movements and the mobilisational impact of the Indian National Congress led to the development of the passive identity of *harijan* and the notion of *uplift* without questioning the caste hierarchy. Poverty and backwardness were significant contributory factors. While the influence of Ambedkar is seen in the late colonial period, it came too late, was limited to a small section of the population and failed to have the tranformative effect it did in Maharashtra."[66]

Hence, the literary expression of this kind of political situation itself becomes a complex and difficult task as it has to narrate and represent several contradictions and complexities which were faced by the society in general and the *Dalit* community in particular. Now we would analyse another novel, Dharti Dhan Na Apana written by Jagdish Chandra that was published in 1972.

Dharati Dhan Na Apana (1972, Novel): Jagdish Chandra

Jagdish Chandra is a prominent literary figure in Hindi literature who has written immensely on torture and exploitation of the oppressed people in the Indian society, especially in Punjab. We find a very sensitive and realistic depiction of the lives of the *Dalits* in his works, which had significant impact on the literary art (though it is to be noted that there is no independent critique of his works except certain literary journalistic criticism).

His major works include *Dharati Dhan Na Apana, Narak Kund Mein Baas* and *Kabhi Na Chhodey Khet* along with other novels and stories. He started writing *Dharati Dhan Na Apana* in Urdu but stopped working on it after initial eight chapters and subsequently completed it in 1968, which got published in 1972. This novel became a milestone, which reflected the socio-eco-political life of the *Dalit* community in Punjab and their exploitation, trauma, struggle, disillusionment, rebellion and failure, which were characteristic of that period (somewhere from late 1960 to early 1970s), for Jagdish Chandra and Hindi literary tradition. Referring to the source of inspiration for this novel, Jagdish Chandra writes, "I got disturbed to witness the plight of the *Dalits* due to poverty and other reasons and the land they were tilling and the houses they resided in were not their own. They had no right on all these resources. My adolescent sensibilities got determination to portray the plight of the lives of these marginalized *Dalits* and "these unforgettable memories and their hidden pain" became the source of inspiration for this novel."[67]

In the Preface of the novel, Jagdish Chandra makes it very clear that he has not experienced "the bitterness of life of the *Harijans*"[68] due to his (upper) caste status but he got the opportunity to witness the trauma of their lives very closely. He further writes, "I have narrated these marginalized characters of Indian life in a very objective and neutral manner and have not attempted to impose my views or ideology throughout the novel."[69] The novel also makes an attempt to narrate inter and intra-community dynamics of the village focussing especially on the plight of the landless *Dalits* and their exploitation, in the Independent state but the feudal Indian society. With this kind of understanding about the lives of the *Dalits*, Jagdish Chandra presented a very important narrative on the contemporary life and its struggle experienced by the *Dalits*.

The novel *Dharati Dhan Na Apana* starts with the return of Kali, the protagonist, to his village in Punjab, which he left six years back due to acute poverty and exploitation and went to Kanpur in Uttar Pradesh to earn his livelihood. He has no parent and relatives except his aunt, Pratapi, who brought him up and with whom he is deeply attached. Kali noticed no change in his village and its life. Same kind of pathetic life for the *Dalits*, same level of exploitation and repression by the upper castes prevailed in the village, rather he found all this much more deeper and intensified.

Local landlords and feuds consider *Dalits* below human beings and treat them in all possible ways of indignity and torture. Chowdhary Harnam Singh, who along with other upper castes exploits *Dalits* economically, politically and emotionally represents the upper caste segment; even the language used by the upper caste is so derogatory and abusive that Kali found intolerable and protested against it. Jagdish Chandra has depicted internalisation of such treatment that continues for centuries in such a way that reader sometimes finds it highly complex to interpret it. For instance, some of the caste men of Kali considered such treatment "as usual" and "normal" (depicted in Chapter III of the novel) and many of them have forcefully submitted to the supremacy of the Chowdharis of the village. But Kali, who returned from the city and has got informed of the political development outside, is not ready to submit like others and decided to lead a dignified and determined life.

Kali endeavours to improve his life and also attempts to instil political consciousness among *Dalits* and through his consistent efforts to unite and provoke them. His first decision to build a *pucca* house becomes a catalyst in the plot. No one in his locality (that has been referred as *'Chamadi'* inappropriately means '*Dalit* Basti') ever owns a *pucca* houses and it was a big decision, not only to visualise but also to execute. It was seen as a challenge to the upper castes, who are rich, own *pucca* house and enjoy all the privileges in the village. Jagdish Chandra seems to use the construction of his house as a metaphor for the construction of new system, a new house that cherishes equality and fraternity where there is no Untouchability and discrimination. There come a lot many problems in the execution of Kali's decision like scarcity of money and raw material. Kali was also made to realise that the land on which he is dreaming to construct a new *pucca* house is a common property of the village, which was donated by the *zamindars* to habitat *Dalits*.[70] There occurs several ups and downs in the realisation of his dream and towards the end of the novel, it remained a dream only leaving him disappointed, distraught and devastated. The money he earned in the city was stolen when he was mourning the death of his aunt and now he lives a lonely life struggling for his dignity.

Kali now attempts to mobilise the *Dalits* on the issue of *'Begar'* and organise them. The novelist has narrated this incident very powerfully, examining inter and intra contradictions of the communities, their lack of political organisation and articulation and also poverty. More than six chapters have been devoted to this incident that investigates very seriously the tensions and contradictions prevalent in the contemporary Indian villages. Issues like political organisation and articulation, mobilisation and agitation, protest and revolt have been dealt in detail highlighting consolidation of the upper castes against the fragmented lower castes who are already disempowered and marginalized in the caste ridden social structures. This episode also addresses various political orientations, which were dominant during the period like reformist, socialist and communist. Though other political orientations have been tackled in a sketchy way the communist orientation has been dealt in detail is being represented by Dr. Bishan Das, who keeps on "harping on the Marxist-Leninist discourse"[71] and attempts to generate some sort of Marxist consciousness among the villagers. *Dalits*, led by Kali, expected total and meaningful support and solidarity from the comrades but they finally got disillusioned with this discourse due to Dr. Bishan Das and others' lack of full support, solidarity and consistency. This led to a compromise between the upper castes and the *Dalits* turning the hope for change in the socio-eco-political set-up in the village and leaving Kali a lone struggler for the cause.

The issues of Untouchability and conversion have also been addressed in the novel. Untouchability is widely practiced in the village and the *Dalits* were humiliated, insulted every day, and are being forced to live a sub-human existence. It has also been portrayed delicately that how conversion from *Dalit* to first, Sikhism and then to Christianity, also failed to bring change in the mindsets of the upper castes. It has been narrated through the life of Nand Singh who first converted to Sikhism and later on to Christianity but upper castes and also his own community members treated him with no difference. He was unable to get a respectable status despite the prosyletization. We find that the conversion to Buddhism movement led by Dr. Ambedkar had powerful impact on the lives of *Dalits* throughout India and people considered it as rejection of Brahmanism but the novelist attempts to portray that without dynamic leadership, high level of political consciousness and political organisation, these movements reach a limitation and restricts itself to limited success.

Kali's relationship with Gyanno becomes the turning point in the novel. Both of them belong to the same caste, community and village where they cannot have marital relationship whatever their emotional and sentimental association. There is a continuous description of this relationship in the text but it get no social approval that led to poisoning of Gyanno by her mother and forcing Kali to leave village, completely defeated, devastated and disillusioned of his dreams, endeavours and vision. The novel starts with his return to the village from city and ends with his tragic and forceful migration to an unknown place.

Dharati Dhan Na Apana portrays the contemporary socio-political realities prevalent during 1970s in our country addressing vital issues, like revolt against Caste System, attack on the practice of Untouchability (despite legal prohibition). It also emphasises on the need for land reforms to empower *Dalits*, especially in the rural area. It becomes evident from the plight of Kali's life and his brethren that unless full-fledged land reforms are introduced in the villages, life for the *Dalits* would not be better. *Dharati Dhan Na Apana* problemaises issue of land reforms and poverty in a very powerful manner and inspires for these grassroots level changes in socio-economic structure to achieve the goal of political and social empowerment.

The novel also attempts to expose the hypocrisy of the socialist and communist orientation adopted by the educated upper castes in the village, (represented by Dr. Bishan Das and his fellows) who sympathetically and notionally supported the cause of the *Dalit* liberation but when it comes to real and genuine solidarity they aligned with their upper castes communities. In this regard, Kali's disillusionment occurred in a process where he visited all possible sources for support from Dr. Bishan Das to Christian priests and others. But all of them refused to support the *Dalits* when they decided to boycott the upper castes Chowdharis. Boycott resulted in a compromise between the *Jats* and the *Dalits*, where later got, in a way, defeated. It happened due to acute poverty that led them to starvation and finally for the compromise. Dr. Bishan Das understood that the *Dalits* have reformist than revolutionary approach but failed to realise that poverty, landlessness and starvation are major obstacles in this direction and failure to address these fundamental issues led for Kali's disillusionment with this approach. Jagdish Chandra also narrates humanistic tendencies, which were existent in the village through the character of Lallu, a wrestler, who is ready to help Kali. But at the same time, the novelist pointed out his limitations to lend full support to the *Dalits*, especially during the boycott.

In this way, we find that *Dharati Dhan Na Apana* is a unique novel on the life of the *Dalits* in an Indian village. It is the first full-length novel on their life portraying socio-eco-cultural and political context, where Kali represents rebellion character of the community, who despite all limitations, contradictions and upper castes dominance, launched the movement for *Dalit* liberation. The failure of the boycott movement is evidently the failure of the in-built exploitative system of Indian society and not the failure of Kali's determination and commitment to the cause. We would see in the subsequent texts that how there is continuity to this spirit and how Kali's vision is becoming successful in due course of the history of the *Dalit* movement in

India.

Nachyo Bahut Gopal (1978, Novel-cum-Reportage): Amrit Lal Nagar

Amrit Lal Nagar (1916-1990) was born in Agra and lived his creative life in and through Lucknow. He inherited literary tradition from the legacy of Premchand and Sharat Chandra, where Premchand inspired him for realistic portrayal of human experiences and Sharat Chandra for self experienced narration of life. These two literary figures had an immense impact on the works and personality of Amrit Lal Nagar, who represented a different tradition in Hindi literature that explores and experimented with the nuances of life and its creative expression blending it with first hand experiences and investigations. His style is also very different, which sometimes makes him a complex novelist and storywriter where he attempted to address numerous issues, interwoven in one plot, and leads analysts for innumerable interpretations. His first story collection, titled *'Vatika'* was published in 1935 and appreciated by Premchand himself, who in response, commented that he expects realistic stories from Amrit Lal Nagar.[72]

It is important to note that the period during which Amrit Lal Nagar was realising his creative self witnessed National Liberation Struggle trade union movement and increased Leftist influence within and outside the Indian National Congress. The first Progressive Writer's Association was held in Lucknow in 1936 with Premchand in the chair, who appealed for a "literature that would generate dynamism, struggle and uneasiness"[73] Dr. Ram Vilas Sharma was also starting advocacy for a committed and progressive literature, which inspired for humanism, progress and harmony. There was also an enhanced Gandhian impact on the socio-political and literary context in the country. In fact, this was the period for redefining our past, shaping our present that explores future India. It was in this context that Amrit Lal Nagar started his creative life and got influenced by all these traits in his writings and subsequently, developed his own distinct style and considered his literature as 'humanist' that is not only emotional but also rational.[74]

In his quest to explore the multifarious contexts of life and its unpredictability, Amrit Lal Nagar wrote on several subjects, expanding the horizon of his creative canvass where he addressed almost every aspect of life, ranging from individual to collective self and from contemporary society to its historical and cultural traditions carried forward from the past.

We can classify his literature in three major streams.[75] The first one is represented by his works like *Mahakaal* (1947), *Boond Aur Samundra* (1956), *Suhaag Ke Nupur* (1960), *Amrit Aur Vish* (1966), *Nachyo Bahut Gopal* (1978) and *Agnigarbha* (1982) where he addressed variety of issues, *e.g.*, problems of middle class and capitalist society, problems of contemporary Indian society, issues related to women's liberation and Untouchability. The second stream is his historical novels as represented by the works like *Karwat* (1985) and *Peedhiya* (1990) that explore impact of colonialism on the Indian society while the third stream represents his cultural and historical novels, for instance, *Ekda Naimisharayane* (1972), *Manas Ka Hans* (1972) and *Khanjan Nayan* (1981). In addition, we find his story collections like *Vatika* (1935), *Aadami, Nahi! Nahi* (1947), *Ek Dil Hazar Daastan* (1955), *Sikandar Har Gaya* (1973) and *Ek Dil Hazar Afsane* (1986) that attempt to address the issues concerning middle class life and its ambitions, expectations, happiness and sorrow, vision and realities. In this way, we find that he endeavoured to touch each and every aspect of contemporary Indian life, especially in the urban scenario, that struggles for meaningful survival amid several limitations.

Portrayal of urban middle class has found special attention in his works and Lucknow became his favourite urban context that synthesises both urban and rural traditions and its majestic *Nawabi* past in its fabric. This emphasis on urban context, hybridising with rural traditions, leads Amrit Lal Nagar towards experimentation with varied themes and concerns. It was in this context that he attempted to write *Nachyo Bahut Gopal* that became sociological documentation on the contemporary life of the *Dalits* living in urban areas. The novel came out after three years of rigorous exploration and is based on surveys, interviews and informal/formal interaction with the community.[76] The style of this work is generally considered as novel-cum-*reportage* as we found several interventions by the author himself in the novel on the issue.

The dedication of the novel is also noteworthy. It has been

dedicated to three personalities, viz, Heera Dom, Mahavir Prasad Dewedi and Jai Prakash Narayan. It is to be noted that Heera Dom is being considered the first poet to express the trauma of his community and Mahavir Prasad Dewedi published his poem in *Saraswati* magazine. The genesis of this work lies in Amrit Lal Nagar's quest to explore the multifarious reality of Indian life as he mentioned in the Preface of the novel that a particular real life incident (where a rich, but aged Brahmin's young wife eloped with a young 'sweeper' man) inspired him to work on this community that was reported in the *Dharmyug* magazine in 1975. We find that the plot of *Nachyo Bahut Gopal* is interwoven on a similar incident, of course, with various creative interventions by the author.

Amrit Lal Nagar makes it clear in the Preface itself that it is his quest to understand the trauma of being a *Dalit* that inspired him to work on such a theme. Here, he made an attempt to explore roots of the problem, investigating it right from the etymological perspective to its historical origin and subsequent development. He quoted from some of the Hindu Scriptures, Dr. Ambedkar and others on this issue and found that "sweepers are not castes and, if at all, they are the caste, then it is a caste of a vanquished."[77] He further elaborated, "Castes, considered Untouchables were, in fact, defeated and humiliated by the victors, who, eccentrically, forced them to do all kinds of menial works."[78] It is with this historical understanding that Amrit Lal Nagar started exploring myths and realities associated with the sweepers community and contextualised the plot of *Nachyo Bahut Gopal* in Lucknow during the mid-1970s.

The plot revolves around Smt. Nirguniya Devi, the central character of the novel, and her life. She is located in a *Dalit* Basti that is representative of her struggle and trauma. Author, through the character of Anshudhar Sharma, endeavours to narrate her life in a very different literary style (by way of push-pull method, where author as well as his characters looks back and forth, sometimes, simultaneously in order to understand both individual and collective self and the contemporary social reality). This distinct method, experimented by Amrit Lal Nagar, makes *Nachyo Bahut Gopal* a novel-cum-*reportage* rather than novel itself. This method also makes the novel a complex one and sometimes, apparent inconsistencies crop up in the form. For instance, *Nachyo Bahut Gopal*, prima facie, looks like a biography of Smt. Nirguniya Devi as told to the journalist author, Anshuman Sharma but repeated interventions on contemporary socio-political dynamics (for example, Chapter 30 referring to Emergency, 1975) by the author makes it reportage, though these references are also intertwined with the main plot of the novel.

Nachyo Bahut Gopal portrays the life of Smt. Nirguniya Devi as the saga of the unpredictability in human life where it is not the birth status that determines one's destiny but rather immense impact of the circumstances which metamorphoses one's life cycle. Smt. Nirguniya spent her childhood (upto 12-13 years) at her maternal grandparents' house amid *Brahamincal* traditions and after their death moved out to the house of her father's employer, Pandit Batuk Prasad, where she was physically exploited by his son and subsequently, married to a seventy five year old man, named Masuriadeen Maharaj.

Her husband, Masuriadeen not only 'policed' her socialisation with the outside world but also restricted her physical mobility and almost kept her 'locked' in his house. Moreover, he was not able to satisfy her sexually. (Chapter 9, page 60). Subsequent development of the events led her to elope with Mohana, the son of their house-sweeper and introduced her with a new world of reality. Mohana takes her to his uncle where she was 'forced' to socialise herself as sweeper and to learn their lifestyle. This transformation has been depicted in such a way by the author that it marked mental agony and trauma of the sweepers' community and their life. This description also substantiates understanding of the author that sweepers were not a caste at all but were subjugated community that was constantly suppressed and humiliated in the course of the history.

Smt. Nirguniya experienced painful transformation and became a sweeper. In due course of time, she became the mother of two children: Nirgun Mohan and Shakuntala. Her husband became a dreaded bandit, who was killed by the police. After his death, she brought up her two children, devoted her life to the service of the community and struggled politically for the right of the *Dalits*. Her daughter, Shakuntala became principal of a college and son, Nirgun Mohan is a government officer in the Press Information Bureau. *Nachyo Bahut Gopal* depicts her struggle for identity, self-respect and rights. We find a very complicated story line in this novel that investigates pathetic lives of the sweepers' community.

The novel is a long one having forty-one chapters in 345 pages depicting almost each and every aspect of human life and addressing crucial issues of the *Dalits*' mobilisation, solidarity, self-respect and identity. In specific, it addresses issue of political consciousness, Ambedkar's movement, Gandhian influence on the lives of *Dalits* (particularly in north India), temple entry movement and mobilisation and consolidation of the *Dalits* for assertion of their rights. It also narrates cultural mobilisation (through celebration of the Ravidas Anniversary), which provided impetus for cultural consolidation of *Dalits* in their quest for equality. Impact of Dr. Ambedkar's movement has been immense, especially among the new generations of the *Dalits*. Smt. Nirguniya's son represents this generation and revolted against caste exploitation and humiliation. He understood caste discrimination as "apartheid"[79] and resolved to fight against it politically and socially.

At the same time, it also attempts to explore the problems faced by a woman, (and when the woman is a *Dalit*) in the male dominated society. She, painfully, said, "none other than women in this world is a slave. I have seen Brahman as well as sweepers, all men are alike…I have experienced the trauma of being *Dalit* in two ways"[80] (one as being a *Dalit* and other as a woman). But, we find high level of political consciousness in the character of Smt. Nirguniya Devi, who, when confronted with the ground realities, rose to assert her rights and resolves to fight against injustice, inequality and exploitation. She not only lives her life with dignity and self-respect but also struggles for her community and their rights, be it Temple Entry or Ravidas Anniversary Celebrations. She emphasises on the importance of education for *Dalits* and their children. Politically, she encourages people for consolidation, solidarity and consistent fight against injustice.

There is a very significant debate running throughout the plot of *Nachyo Bahut Gopal*. This debate pointed out towards the origin of the sweeper castes. Author makes an attempt to find out the historical reasons for the origin of this caste but found that there is no caste as sweeper *per se*, but historically, the victors forced vanquished to do menial jobs and subsequently, they were identified as sweepers and were considered lower castes.

This understanding led author to conceptualise the character of Smt. Nirguniya Devi, who spent her childhood amidst the *Brahamin* surroundings, and metamorphoses to a *Dalit* by a series of development in her life, where she becomes victim of the social structure and its predicament. What is important is to recognise the fact that she accepts her 'identity' and resolves to live it with dignity and self-respect as she emphasised, "I would like to be in the same society, I even don't have a desire to become a *Brahmani* again."[81] This indicates her self-dignity and commitment to the cause of *Dalit* upliftment. Here it is to be noted that some critics argued that Smt. Nirguniya's efforts for *Dalit* emancipation are noteworthy and her love with Mohana transforms her to a sweeper. Nirguniya adapts to a sweeper's lifestyle under pressure in the same way as the *Dalits* are forced to do *Begari* and other menial jobs and these kinds of circumstances are not comfortable. Her (upper caste) past always remained with her at least on a subterranean level.[82] But this also pointed out that there is no sweeper caste *per se* but it is caste-ridden social structure that has forced one section of the society to be considered as lower castes and *Dalits*.

In this way, we find that *Nachyo Bahut Gopal* investigates several causes for the problem and addresses vital issues of the *Dalit* identity, mobilisation and empowerment. The novel also highlights psychological trauma experienced by the *Dalit* community in a caste-ridden society where they have been systematically marginalized. It also focuses on the *Dalit* assertion through community formation and launching a struggle against injustice, inequality and discrimination. It envisions that "freedom/independence are the best cherished goals…there are two kinds of people who are slave: one, women and the other, sweepers. Till the moment these people are slave, any kind of freedom remains a total farce."[83]

Mahabhoj (1979 Novel): Mannu Bhandari

Another novel that came up in 1979 was *Mahabhoj* (The Great Feast) authored by Mannu Bhandari, which comments on socio-eco-political structures, erosion of values, political corruption and precarious life conditions of the *Dalits*.

Mannu Bhandari started her creative journey as storywriter with several story collections like *Main Har Gayee* (1957), *Teen Nigahon Ki Tasveer* (1958), *Yahi Sach Hai* (1966), *Eke Plate Sailab* (1968) and *Trishanku* (1978). These stories addressed women's issues, contradictions of middle class family life, their aspirations and expectations. Mannu Bhandari also wrote some novels like *Eke Inch Muskan* (1961), *Aapka Bunty* (1971) and *Mahabhoj* (1979) where *Mahabhoj* became her most important contribution to the Hindi literary field that proved powerful statement on the contemporary social and political system during 1970s.

Author drew inspiration for *Mahabhoj* from the contemporary environment that characterised by erosion of democratic values, level of inhuman treatment to the lower strata of Indian society and political manipulation for *Realpolitik*. Mannu Bhandari herself mentioned in the beginning of the novel, "it seems to me that it is very important, comfortable and reassuring to observe the interior drama of one's life, to consider one's personal distress and inner turmoil. But when one's own house is on fire, confining oneself to one's inner world and giving expression to only that, appears irrelevant, ridiculous and to some extent indecent. It is perhaps this consideration that underlies the creation of this novel. I look upon this work as an expression of the debt I owe to the environment which has determined my personality and my destiny."[84] In addition, author also drew inspiration from the *Belachi* Massacre in Patna district happened on May 27, 1979 where 14 *Dalits*, including two children, were killed. This Massacre threatened the very conscience of a fearless democracy, its governance and administration. Mannu Bhandari took this incident as a reference point to evolve a political novel underlining numerous issues of Indian democracy (democratic values, political parties, elections and political opportunism) and its role for the betterment of the lives of the *Dalits* in India.

Contemporary developments in political environment took Mannu Bhandari to "venture out from the subjective world of her previous fiction into the realities of grassroots politics in India–the political give and take, the strategic moves and counter-moves likened to a game of chess with the very lives of the constituents its pawns, and a Machiavellian grasp of the terms of political power... *Mahabhoj* is quite simply a tale of the betrayal of public trust for private ends."[85] "The novel opens with the mysterious death of a village boy (Bisu), an insignificant event which takes greater implications as members of the opposing parties in an important by-elections feast upon the tragedy like the Brahmin priests at the death-rites banquet; hence the title. Humanitarian concerns as thus orchestrated by a political framework which gives the work its structure… *Mahabhoj* is first, though not foremost, a primer for the aspiring politician, cataloguing the mechanics of political success, the measures and counter measures taken by the rivals–the grassroots political process transformed into thinly disguised fiction. Its structure is the chess game: the alternating moves of two adept players, with no final solution in sight. The rules of the game are the principles to be followed, the political courses more expedient than exemplary."[86] This kind of plot structure makes *Mahabhoj* a political novel that critically examines entire political system addressing various issues through complicated problematization and leaves out for the reader to explore solutions to the problem.

The plot revolves around the murder of Bisu, whose dead body was found in outskirts of the village called *Saroha*, where by-elections are due very soon. Bisu's murder makes this by-election a playground for two parties: one, ruling party led by Da Sahib and the other opposing one represented by Sukul Babu, who is also contesting elections from this constituency. This murder draws special attention not because of the fact that Bisu belonged to the *Dalit* community but his murder became the central agenda for both the parties for acquiring political power. As is being mentioned in the text, "In truth, there was nothing special about the man or the incident. It was simply a matter of coincidence, place and time synchronized by an event important enough to stir even *Saroha*. In a month-and-a-half there would be an election, a by-election for just one seat in the Legislature, to be sure. But it was still important, for contesting it was the former Chief Minister, Sukul Babu, representing all the parties defeated in the last election, protesting, challenging the very existence of the ruling party… It was Sukul Babu's candidacy that gave the election importance. Just one seat, but so critical for the whole Cabinet. All events thus had greater implications. On any other day what would Bisu or his death have meant?"[87]

Mahabhoj narrates all kinds of political manipulations (even merciless death of an innocent) employed by the political leaders to gain and maintain political power. But it is to be noted that the author writes about the whole political system and its complicated nitty-gritty in such a way to make it clear and precise without any special emphasis that politicians have betrayed public trust and lost even minimum respect to human dignity, democratic values, principles of natural justice and morality for the sake of political power and opportunism.

There are two important characters in the novel: Da Sahib and Sukul Babu. Da Sahib, who is the current Chief Minister, is being portrayed, apparently with clean image and principled leadership, who displays great respect to democracy, freedom of press, proper governance and corruption free administration. But his political expediencies convey a different message for example his interview to the editor of the *Mashaal* newspaper and subsequently doubling its newsprint paper quota, introducing Cottage Industry Plan just before the elections and its inauguration by Bisu's father from *Saroha* village. All these expedient tactics, adopted by Da Sahib, manifest completely different impact that suggests how political manipulations and manoeuvrings are used opportunistically even by an apparent clean image principled leader. Sukul Babu is the former Chief Minister who is contesting by-elections after the defeat of his party during last general elections. He ruled for about ten years with absolute power and no challenge to his leadership. It is to be noted that Bisu was arrested during his tenure without any reason and mercilessly tortured that traumatised him till his death but now Sukul Babu is very sympathetic for Bisu and pledged to punish the guilty responsible for this act. In this context, it should also be noted down that by-elections, otherwise, would have been a very insignificant event but Bisu's murder gave both the leaders an opportunistic agenda and the entire sequence of development changed so fast, thus making this incident a reference point for the whole novel. He utilises all means to win this by-election and in the process shrewdly attempts to seize the opportunity for political power that is being portrayed as *Realpolitik* throughout the novel.

Mahabhoj also portrays the practice of defection and political opportunism. Trilochan (Lochan *Bhaiyya*), who defected to Da Sahib after Sukul Babu's defeat in last elections, gains political power and represents this tendency that started manifesting in the contemporary Indian political system. Along with many other tendencies being reflected in the novel, *Mahabhoj* attempts to critically portray almost every character that contributes to the successful governance of Indian democratic polity like, political leaders (Da *Sahib*, Sukul Babu, Trilochan, Rao, Chowdhary, Appa *Sahib*), journalists (Datta Babu), Police (DIG, Saxena), helpless peasants, *Dalits* and local pressure groups as well as caste struggle (represented by Thakur v/s *Dalits* conflict in the village). The novel also narrates struggle for justice led by Binda and Rukma who were tortured through systemic flaws but continued their fight.

In this way, *Mahabhoj* becomes "typical of the political novel genre, it offers no solution. Rather, it dramatically brings forward the modern ideologies, expediencies and current realities in conflict with the traditional morals by which India has defined herself as a nation and people…The political concerns which enter an author's life, both public and imaginative, may often transform every aspect of his creative work–language, style, imagery, form. As such is the case with Mannu Bhandari's *Mahabhoj* in which the author has ventured out into an area of social criticism through a striking simplicity of language difficult in translation, a crude realistic vitality and a genuine concern for the Indian moral tradition…The novel is rather a realistic chronicle of the behaviour patterns of highly political groups. It is a gallery of types: exploited peasants and outcastes squeezed by poverty, powerful landowners and corrupt politicians, and stirred to occasional action only by outside stimulations; tainted idealists whose eclipses are caused by acting in accordance with their conscience rather than the Party or power structure; the perverters of power, demagogues with messianic complexes or gangsters ruling by the ballot; and the committed revolutionary."[88] The conflict between political power, moral values and democratic principles remains a running thread throughout the novel and it explores to investigate these concepts in grassroots level reality that is characterised by erosion of values, political opportunism, manipulation, manoeuvring, muscle power and corruption in the administration of the country and these factors keep the *Dalits* at a disadvantaged level where they are already marginalized by Caste System and discrimination. This kind of literary exploration leads towards serious introspection and inward looking; recognizing principles of Equality, Liberty and Solidarity for all human beings.

Thus examined, we find that *Mahabhoj*'s contribution to the

Hindi literary expression is important in terms of highlighting flaws, which are inbuilt in the political system, and keeping the *Dalits* discriminated and marginalized. It is important to address systemic flaws (of a democratic polity) and to investigate why this system has not delivered expected results, especially for the upliftment of the *Dalits*, as visualised by the Founding Fathers of the Constitution of India. *Mahabhoj* proves to be an attempt in this direction and brings this issue to the centrality of Hindi literary tradition.

NOTES

1. Omvedt, Gaid. *Ibid.* p. 161.
2. Please see Gooptu, Nandini. *Ibid.* p. 277-298 for further detail.
3. *'Raj'*, Rajpal Singh. *Swami Achuutanand aur Unka Sahitya* in Jai Prakash Kardam (ed.) *Dalits Sahitya*, 1999 (Delhi, Publisher not mentioned, 1999) p. 67.
4. Please see *People's Art in the Twentieth Century: Theory and Practice* (Delhi: Jan Natya Manch, July 1999-September 2000) p. 73.
5. Premchand. *Sahitya Ka Uddeshya* (Presidential Address at the First Conference of Progressive Writer's Association in April 1936).
6. *Ibid.*
7. *Ibid.*
8. *Ibid.*
9. Mukherjee, Meenakshi. *Realism and Reality: The Novel and Society in India* (Delhi: Oxford University Press, 1985) p. 146.
10. Premchand. *Kafan* from Bhishma Sahni (ed.) *Pratinidhi Kahaniyan* (Delhi: Rajkamal Prakashan, 1987) p. 138.
11. Mukherjee, Meenakshi. *Ibid.* p. 146.
12. *Ibid.* p. 146.
13. Premchand. Presidential Address. *Ibid.*
14. *Ibid.*
15. *Ibid.*
16. Mukherjee, Meenakshi. *Ibid.* p. 147.
17. Sahni, Bhisma. *As Story Writer* in Nagendra (ed.) *Premchand: An Anthology* (Delhi: Bansal & Co., 1981) p. 140.
18. *Ibid.* p. 141.
19. Chaudhry, Surendra. *Kafan* in Markandya and Satya Prakash Mishra (ed.) *Premchand Ki Kahaniyon Ka Mahatav* (Allahabad: Sumit Prakashan, 1998) p. 20.
20. Gupta, Shanti Swarup. *Premchand's Works: A Chronological Survey* in Nagendra, *Ibid.* p. 55.
21. Mukherjee, Meenakshi. *Ibid.* p. 146.

22. Singh, Harbhajan. *Art of Premchand* in Nagendra. *Ibid.* p. 125.
23. *Ibid.*
24. Bharati, Kanwal. *Dalit Sahitya aur Premchand* in Sadanand Sahi (ed.) *Dalit Sahitya ki Avdharna aur Premchand* (Gorakhpur: Premchand Sahitya Sansthan, 2000) p. 87-88.
25. *Ibid.* p. 89.
26. *Ibid.* p. 89.
27. *Bechain*, Shyoraj Singh. *Dalit Sahitya Ki Avdharana aur Premchand Ka Chamar Chitran* in Sadanand Sahi (ed.) *Ibid.* p. 110.
28. Bharati, Kanwal. *Gair Dalit Lekhako Ke Dalit Sahitya Par Hamle...* in Jai Prakash Kardam (ed.) *Dalit Sahitya* 2000 (Delhi: publisher not mentioned, 2000) p. 194.
29. Bharati, Kanwal. *Dalit Sahitya aur Premchand* in Sadanand Sahi (ed.) *Ibid.* p. 92.
30. *Ibid.* p. 98.
31. Pandey, Manager. *Ibid.* p. 290-91.
32. Nagendra. *Premchand: Reviewed* in Nagendra (ed.) *Ibid.* p. 5.
33. Hasan, Mohammad. *The Art of Novel in* Nagendra (ed.) *Ibid.* p. 105.
34. Pandey, Manager. *Ibid.* 293.
35. Hasan, Mohammad. *Ibid.* p. 102-103.
36. Premchand. Presidential Address. *Ibid.*
37. Mukherjee, Meenakshi. *Ibid.* p. 148.
38. *Ibid.* p. 162.
39. *Ibid.* p. 163.
40. *Ibid.* p. 163.
41. *Ibid.* p. 149.
42. *Ibid.* p. 149.
43. *Ibid.* p. 149.
44. Singh, Harbhajan. *Ibid.* p. 126-127.
45. Premchand. *Godan* (translated by Jai Ratan and P. Lal) (Bombay: Jaico Publishing House, eleventh impression, 1991) p. 142.
46. Premchand. *Godan.* p. 202.
47. *Ibid* p. 202.
48. *Ibid.* p. 202.
49. *Ibid.* p. 203.
50. *Ibid.* p. 203.
51. *Ibid.* p. 203.
52. *Ibid.* p. 203-204.
53. *Ibid.* p. 204.
54. *Ibid.* p. 207.
55. *Ibid.* p. 273.
56. *Ibid.* p. 274.
57. *Ibid.* p. 274.
58. *Ibid.* p. 275.
59. *Ibid.* p. 275.

60. Sahi, Sadanand. *Godan Mein Dalit Prasang Ke Nehitarth* (Gorakhpur: Premchand Sahitya Sanstha, year not mentioned) p. 8.
61. Mukherjee, Meenakshi. *Ibid.* p. 164.
62. *Ibid.* p. 165.
63. Zelliot, Eleanor. *Ibid.* p. 219.
64. *Ibid.* p. 180.
65. *Ibid.* p. 211.
66. Pai, Sudha. Notes from the paper on *Understanding Dalit Identity in Uttar Pradesh: Emergence, Forms and Impact*, presented at the National Seminar on *Dalits*, Identity and the Mainstream: An Interrogation on August 29-31, 2001 at Centre for Social Studies, Surat.
67. Chandra, Jagdish. *Dharati Dhan Na Apana* (Delhi: Rajkamal Prakashan, first pub. 1972) p. 7-8.
68. *Ibid.* p. 8.
69. *Ibid.* p. 8.
70. *Ibid.* p. 55.
71. *Ibid.* p. 110.
72. Please see Chaube, Devendra. *Kathakar Amrit Lal Nagar* (Delhi: Jagat Ram & Sons, 1994) for further detail.
73. Mukherjee, Meenakshi. *Ibid.* p. 145.
74. Chaube, Devendra. *Ibid.* p. 144.
75. *Ibid.* p. 144.
76. Nagar, Amril Lal. *Nachyo Bahut Gopal* (Delhi: Rajpal & Sons, 1999 edition) Preface.
77. *Ibid.*
78. *Ibid.*
79. I*bid.* p. 34.
80. *Ibid.* p. 229.
81. *Ibid.* p. 55.
82. Kardam, Jai Prakash. *Dalit Vishyak Hindi Upanayas-Ek Drishti* in Yudhrat Aam Aadami (Hazaribagh: January-June, 1998) p. 30.
83. Nagar, Amril Lal. *Ibid.* p. 343.
84. Bhandari, Mannu. *Mahabhoj* (translated 'The Great Feast' by Richard Alan Williams) (Delhi: Radha Krishna Prakashan, 1981) Note preceding the Novel.
85. Williams, Richard Allan. (Translator) *Ibid.* p. 7.
86. *Ibid.* p. 143-44.
87. Bhandari, Mannu. *Ibid.* p. 11.
88. Williams, Richard Allan. *Ibid.* p. 145.

5

Mohan Dass Naimishray to Recent Writings Towards Empowerment

It is important to note that there occurred a process of consolidation of the *Dalits* in northern part of India during 1980s with two inter-linked processes, visible from the mid-1960s: first was the defeat and temporary decline of the Congress after the 1967 elections and the second process marked entry of the middle and Backward Classes (BCs) mobilised by the Opposition parties, such as BKD, into politics. Then onwards, formation of Bahujan Samaj Party (BSP) in 1984 further consolidated the *Dalit* community with increased political mobilisation and consciousness and bringing the deprived section along with minorities to a common platform. Formation of BSP is being seen as a culmination of Kanshi Ram's efforts in this direction through the Backward and Minorities Communities Employees Federation (BAMCEF) and the *Dalits Shoshit Samaj Sangharsh Samiti* (DS-4), which helped the *Dalits* to assert them independently and autonomously. From 1989, BSP started contesting State Assembly Elections with 13 seats and reached its best to 98 in UP 2002 Elections. This clearly manifests its hold over the community and now it is an important political player in the politics of Uttar Pradesh pushing forward its *Bahujan* agenda.

Hence, the *Dalit* assertion in India, especially northern India has gone through continuous mobilisation and participation enhancing political consciousness among the *Dalits* that ensured their political participation in governance of the country. This also ensured the formation of the *Dalit* identity in north India, particularly in U.P. Commenting on *Dalit* identity, Sudha Pai writes, "the gradual emergence of *Dalit* consciousness and movements was a significant feature of colonial India. The pace of change was however, different in different regions leading to uneven development of the *Dalit* movement across the subcontinent in the post-Independence period. While parts of colonial Southern and Western India experienced strong movement demanding reservations and improved social status under leaders such as B.R. Ambedkar and M.C. Rajah, these were conspicuous by their absence in most parts of North India. In UP, the lack of an anti-caste ideology or social reform movements and the mobilisational impact of the Indian National Congress led to the development of the passive identity of *harijan* and the notion of uplift without questioning the caste hierarchy... (now during the recent times) *Dalit* identity has two faces, neither of which can be described as revolutionary. One under the leadership of the BSP believes that capturing state power and introducing policies favourable to *Dalits* from above can best serve *Dalit* upliftment. It is elitist, conservative and election-oriented and aims at political empowerment of *Dalits*. The other represented by the micro-level process of Ambedkarisation functions within civil society to protect the interests of *Dalits* through collective social organisations. It believes that spreading the message of Ambedkar through various methods of grassroots mobilisation such as education and building awareness will in time introduce social transformation."[1] It is in this regard that the new wave of *Dalit* literature came up in the Hindi belt during late 1980s and we find that it has a new energy questioning the very foundation of the caste system. This protest literature that is being led by the educated *Dalit* writer-activists enthused fresh enthusiasm among the community and political changes in the region also complimented their efforts, thus making *Dalit* literature a catalyst in the on-going *Dalit* assertion/ movement for mobilisation, identity and empowerment.

It is with this understanding that we would analyse Hindi *Dalit* literature that came up during 1990s and made a great impact on the formation of *Dalit* identity, its consolidation with increased level of political consciousness and its heading for empowerment: social, economic and political. It should also be mentioned that these writings proved very crucial in the development of Hindi literature itself as these questioned the prevalent elitism, upper-caste domination, unrealistic linguistic sophistication (having no resemblance with ground realities) and parameters for literary aesthetics sense. In this direction, we would first analyse *Apne Apne Pinjare*, the first *Dalit* autobiography in Hindi, by Mohan Dass Naimishray.

Apne Apne Pinjare (1995, Autobiography): Mohan Dass Naimishray

Apne Apne Pinjare is being considered the first autobiography in the Hindi *Dalit* Literature and narrates prevalent level of exploitation and life conditions of the *Dalit* community in a very intensive and sensitive manner. This autobiography becomes an important first hand documentation of pathetic conditions faced by the *Dalit* community in Meerut (Uttar Pradesh) where Mohan Dass Naimishray was born and where by experienced social, economic and political exploitation. This is the story right from the childhood to adulthood (roughly upto the age of 20–22 years). Overall style of the autobiography is novel-like and explains in detail the geographical settlement of the *Dalit* community in Meerut city as well as during the community festivals like *Ganga Mela*. At the same time, author questions time and again the caste system, Brahmanism and unequal economic system. In fact, his autobiography is the development of a child, who is being told about his caste status repeatedly and gradually becomes conscious of his surroundings that make him politically conscious person who questions all levels of exploitation. In this way, *Apne Apne Pinjare* proves to be a significant landmark in the evolution of the Hindi *Dalit* Literature.

Apne Apne Pinjare can be analysed in two conceptual categories: one, the first hand literary expression of contemporary socio-economic-political and cultural contexts around the author and two, impact of these situations on his development. We would analyse these categories in subsequent four sub-categories, *viz.*,

Socio-economic Context

Apne Apne Pinjare begins with detail narration of Meerut city. It referred to almost every aspect of human life ranging from historical instances to contemporary life styles of the inhabitants to its cultural richness. Whereas the author mentions the impact of 1857, visit of Jawaharlal Nehru, B.R. Ambedkar, Sheikh Abdullah, Jagjivan Ram, B.P. Maurya and others indicating political history and tradition of the town, he also took care to mention geographic settlement of different communities, their occupations, food habits and cultural traits.

The author is born in Meerut city whose "geography is changing but history remains constant"[2] (*Shahr ka Bhoogol badal raha tha. Par Itihas vaisa hi tha.*) He lost his mother during his early childhood and his uncle and aunt brought him up. Born in a *Dalit* family, author along with his family (uncle and aunt) experience innumerable difficulties and torture to have a dignified social existence. Caste status becomes the only identity of a child right from his birth as Mohan Dass Naimishray wrote, "we were enslaved centuries after centuries. The moment a child is born, s/he is destined with his or her caste. The caste becomes child's sole identity."[3] He further elaborated, "We were subjected to humiliation since a long time though we were not culprits (*Gunahagaar*). We were defeated people pushed back on the margin by the Aryans. We did not have decorations, medals and prizes by the Britishers. What we have is a bitter past and wounded experience. These wounds get resurfaced when body and soul are being hurt. We were cut off from our own history after being marginalized for centuries. We were subject to forget our culture. Our weapons got blunted. First we were displaced our settlements (*Bastis*) and later on from our culture."[4]

Here we find a resemblance of views with *Nachyo Bahut Gopal*'s concluding remarks where Amrit Lal Nagar writes, "*Dalits* are not any caste. Victors forced the vanquished to do menial jobs."[5] We also find a common thread in the demand expressed by both the character in these literary work whereas in *Apne Apne Pinjare*, Mohan Dass Naimishray questioned the very foundation of Hindu society when he writes, "how cruel was that history and culture…which we have inherited for so long"[6] and *Nachyo Bahut Gopal*'s Nirguniya Devi asked for structural changes in society so that life conditions of the *Dalits* could improve and they could live with dignity.

Narrating historical reasons for depravity and exploitation, Mohan Dass Naimishray proceeded to explain the prevalent socio-economic structure the and inter community interaction, particularly with the Muslim community. Author depict tension and frenzy that pervades during communal riots between two communities and brings *Dalits* under the umbrella of Hindu fold that brings inconvenient feelings in the minds of the author as a young child.[7] This feeling urged author to know more about his origin as an individual, caste and community that percolates a feeling of community and consciousness. Here that subjective elements as well as the objective cognition of the contemporary situation becomes important for generation of a sense of community and community consciousness. This is also the beginning of the generation of political consciousness among the *Dalits* where they become subject to repeated humiliation who atrocities and are being 'reminded' of their lower status.

Economic conditions of the *Dalit* families were pathetic. They were heavily indebted and dependent on the wishes of the upper castes for getting loans that attaches high rate of interest. These loans keep on multiplying even after paying back the principal amount with interest, with the cunning manipulation of the upper castes. This makes loan a vicious cycle that never ends for the *Dalits* and their families. An iconic example of this situation could be found in Premchand's *Godan* that we have already discussed. In *Apne Apne Pinjare* this is a continuation of the same cycle that makes economic conditions of the *Dalits* worse and pathetic making life doubly difficult for the community as Mohan Dass Naimishray expressed in the following line, "our life gets surrounded by so many difficulties including *Begar*. If we don't perform *Begar* our life becomes encompassed by difficulties and problems...we have double burden: one is the burden of poverty and another is that of Caste."[8]

Cultural Context

Cultural context is depicted through community festivals, rituals and community feast in the *Apne Apne Pinjare*. There is reference to the *Ravidas Jayanti* celebration and its festive preparation by the *Dalits* community in this part of the country. *Ravidas Jayanti* is celebrated with gaiety every year throughout northern India.

This is a community festival and makes *Dalits* organise themselves through cultural celebrations. This festival also serves the purpose of instilling a sense of commonality among the community making them organised also. Mohan Dass Naimishray himself participated in one of the *Ravidas Jayanti* celebrations and feels happy about it as this provides him a chance to be distinct from the Hindu religious celebrations, where *Dalits* are not allowed to participate. The *Dalits* were also discriminated in the Hindu temples as Mohan Dass Naimishray expressed that "we were *Shudras* for temples and upper castes. We were untouchables. We were *Dalits* but not human beings. Even our shadow was contaminating for the upper castes."[9] In this situation, *Ravidas Jayanti* provides *Dalits* an opportunity to have their own symbolism and thereby translating it into an identity as opposed to Hindu religious celebrations. Further, there is also reference to the *Ganga Mela* on the bank of the Ganges but caste discrimination is also prevalent there and there is discriminatory settlement arrangement for the lower castes.

Mohan Dass Naimishray has also mentioned about the community feast during marriage among the *Dalit* community. He has narrated miserable conditions prevalent among the community and their cultural functions. He writes, "no one from the upper castes has ever attended our marriage parties…"[10] and the party is in progress on the pavement of the roads passer-by often make remarks like *"abe dekh, Chamaron ke chawal, chmaron ki dal, chamaron ke laddoo…*"[11] (Oh, see, rice of the *Dalits*, pulses of the *Dalits*, sweets of the *Dalits*…)

In this way, caste status becomes the only parameter for the community that determines the very life conditions of people. It gets manifested in every aspects of their life and becomes a permanent feature for their identity. Author finds it problematic and attempts to revolt against it right from the childhood when he boycotted Hindu temples after being humiliated by the priest as he said, *"thuu, tuhara mandir aur tuhara prasad…*"[12] (Hell with your temple and its offerings). Further, he feels throughout his autobiographical narration that caste identity becomes very prominent throughout the life of an individual and even after his death, as he mentioned, *"aadami jab paida hota uski jaati likhai jati hai aur marne par bhi."*[13] (When a person is born his caste is mentioned and also after his death)

Political Context

The Republican Party and the Socialist Party depict levels of political participation among the Dalits through municipal elections, political meetings. Mohan Dass Naimishray's uncle, Ram Prasad (Ba) contested municipality elections and won to become a member with the support of the community. He campaigned in a very low manner and his campaign was more personalised. The whole community celebrated his victory and people address him as *'Member Sahib'* and his wife as *'Membarani'*. Mohan Dass Naimishray noticed marginal change of attitude (in terms of respect) towards his Ba but his is limited to his own community as he writes, "Community people started paying much respect to Ba but he remains as earlier (read *Dalit*) for the other castes: *din bhar chamda kutene ya pitane wals chamar, mochi*."[14] (a cobbler who works out throughout the day with leather).

There is also reference to Ambedkar's death and its influence in this town. People mourned his death throughout India including Meerut and Mohan Dass Naimishray came to know about his death from his Ba and started thinking about him. This is the beginning of this political initiation and socialisation when he encounters with the ideals of Baba Saheb Ambedkar through his family members. Though he was not able to make out much as a child, he started thinking about Dr. Ambedkar. Dr. Ambedkar visited Meerut twice and addressed at the *Bhaisali* Ground and Meerut College. When Dr. Ambedkar's ashes were brought to Meerut, Mohan Dass Naimishray mention that this brought a sense of consciousness among the community as he writes, "the sun of consciousness started rising high among the community. Their dormant feelings got awakened. Our locality was honoured by paying tributes to Dr. Ambedkar's ashes, which were kept in the *Panchayat Bhawan*. This also brought honour to our locality in the whole district."[15] Name of the *Panchayat Bhawan* was also changed to *Baba Saheb Dr. Ambedkar Bhawan* in his memory.

Then the political environment of the town was changing with meetings of the *Dalit* leaders like B.P. Maurya from Republican Party of India, Maharaj Singh Bharti, Pyarelal, Mani Ram Bagadi and Manjoor Ahmed from the Socialist Party and Babu Jagjivan Ram. Pointing out to the changing political scenario, Mohan Dass Naimishray writes, "the winds of change were high in Meerut...Though people form this locality were influenced by the Congress right from the beginning but now Republican Party has also started making inroads among the community. We used to campaign during elections (though as child). This was the period of renaissance for the people of our community. We were gradually discarding centuries old slavery."[16]

Thus we find that political consciousness was increasing among the *Dalits* in Meerut during these days and as a child Mohan Dass

Naimishray was initiated into political socialisation and participation. This also indicates that community was becoming aware of their rights and rising against exploitation and fighting for dignity and equality.

Though the socio-eco-politico-cultural life of the *Dalits* is changing but marginally caste remains the only identity for the *Dalits*. Mohan Dass Naimishray has critically narrated 'what it means to be a member of the *Dalit* community' in his autobiographical narration. Level of humiliation and exploitation faced by him, in fact, represent large section of the *Dalit* community and he has given first hand sensitive account of life conditions that a *Dalit* is subjected to. It also reveals the very course of development of a child (in terms of psychological, political and philosophical development) who is right from his birth subject to caste exploitation and humiliation. His caste status determines every thing in his life though Mohan Dass Naimishray has noticed that there is no caste identity in the metropolitan towns like Bombay. He writes, "There was hunger, poverty and unemployment in Bombay but there were no caste boundaries among people. No one asked my caste, though the name of my native place was asked. I liked it for the first time. Women in this city get identity by their costume, attitude and gesture not by their castes. There were no castes (read casteism) in metropolitan towns. Man is a man and woman is a woman."[17] In this way, Mohan Dass Naimishray finds some change of attitude in metropolitan towns where he found that caste is not the only identity of an individual.

Mohan Dass Naimishray narrated early years of his life in *Apne Apne Pinjare* spanning for about early twenty years. The narration style of the autobiography is novel-like that depicts numerous things like the community, town, inter-community social relations, cultural and religious festivals, rituals and many other. In this way, it also becomes a documentation of life and its struggle (which has been comprehensively covered by the author) that highlights almost entire world of things happening in and around the town.

This also becomes clear by having a look on the Dedication of the book by the author where he says, "a black and white document of struggle of my life, dedicated to all those who got associated and disassociated with me having feelings of happiness and sorrow."[18] The running thread throughout the text is caste status and its impact on the life of the author and by extension on the community. It has also questioned the very foundation of the Hindu society and in the process challenged them also.

Critics have viewed *Apne Apne Pinjare* from a variety of perspectives but every one appreciated author's effort to narrate first hand account of the *Dalit* community. It is precisely due to this reason that makes *Apne Apne Pinjare* the first autobiography in Hindi by a *Dalit* himself. There has been some criticism also to the style of narration as well as its form. Use of abusive language is also criticised. But Mohan Dass Naimishray said in an interview that he has used the language spoken by the *Dalits* so that narrative could be realistic and effective.[19] Author has used regional variation of the language and also mentioned several proverbs used by the *Dalits* during their daily interaction. Since the context is largely semi-urban, the language is also a mixture of rural and urban linguistic categories.

Some critics have criticised *Apne Apne Pinjare* in terms of its usages, for instance, Rajat Rani 'Meenu' considers some of the references in the Autobiography "irrelevant and out of context events, like references to impotent brother, prostitutes, infatuation of teen aged sisters in Bombay etc."[20] Depiction of women has also been criticised by some critics.

Thus, it may be said that *Apne Apne Pinjare* becomes an important contribution to literary tradition of Hindi *Dalit* Literature and inspires many *Dalits* to write their autobiographies and first hand experiences. In this way, *Apne Apne Pinjare* proved to be a significant milestone for the contemporary Hindi *Dalit* Literature.

Kranti Shesh Hai **(1995, Poetry): Lalchand** ***'Rahi'***

This is a collection of forty-two poems on the *Dalit* emancipation composed by Lalchand *'Rahi'* published by the Madhya Pradesh *Dalit* Sahitya Academy, in 1995. "This collection has touched almost every aspect of the *Dalit* community. On the one hand, it expresses socio-eco-political conditions of the community and on the other depicts their religious aspects also."[21] In Preface, the poet has clearly mentioned that movement against oppression and exploitation is his responsibility and he finds poetic expression, as a weapon, in this movement. He draws inspiration from Buddha, Kabir, Ravidas,

Mahatma Phule and Dr. Ambedkar and considers his contribution to the movement against caste exploitation as his responsibility. This approach manifests his political understanding and makes him a politically conscious person who is contributing to the movement through his poetry and other literary works. We would discuss some of his poetry from this collection.

Giving a clarion call to the *Dalits*, Lalchand *'Rahi'* writes:
Break the chains of traditions
Leave the rotten path (of the upper castes)
Because, breaking old prison of traditions
may lead to a significant endeavour
For *Dalits*, in form of
Education
Organisation, and
Agitation[22]
(Leek Se Hato in *Kranti Shesh Hai*)

It is to be noted that the words used by the poet towards the end of this poem are Education, Organisation and Agitation. These are the same words Dr. Ambedkar used in many of this speeches and writings.

In the title poem, *Kranti Shesh Hai*, Lalchand *'Rahi'* while recognising contributions made by the *Dalits* in the National Liberation Movement, questioned inequality prevalent in Independent India. He writes:

Only fifteen percent got
Sweetness of Independence
But eighty five percent
remain on margins
Revolution is yet to come
for
Equality and Dignity
for
The Right to live with Dignity for *Dalit*[23]
(*Kranti Shesh Hai*)

This poem indicates the political scenario that is prevalent in modern India where upper castes are enjoying fruits of Independence while it is still exploitative system for *Dalits* with unequal economic structures and caste oppression.

There is another poem that reasserts political principles of the *Dalit* movement redefining socio-political identity.

> I can say it
> My thinking is fighting (against)
> and would continue to fight with their (upper caste) thinking
> till
> The reestablishment of my existence and identity[24]
> (Yudhrat Soch in *Kranti Shesh Haí*)

In this way, we find that the poetic expression of political consciousness among *Dalits* is very articulate and questions caste oppression and economic exploitation. It is to be noted that the poet belongs to Madhya Pradesh and we can find similar feelings among *Dalits* throughout the country. As far as the style of this collection is concerned, it is very easy and communicable appealing directly to the community to rise against exploitation. There is also a sense of responsibility that demonstrates high level of political consciousness in author as well as his poems. This kind of literary works make Hindi *Dalit* Literature a political literature with principles of equality, dignity and solidarity as its foundation.

***Suno Brahaman* (1996, Poetry): Malkhan Singh**

Suno Brahaman is another collection of representative *Dalit* poetry composed by Malkhan Singh that got published in 1996 from Rampur (Uttar Pradesh). This is a collection of sixteen poems on the life and its struggle of the *Dalit* community. Prevalence of casteism, untouchability, exploitation, atrocities and hypocrisy forced poet to revolt against this system and he adopted poetic literary expression as a means to protests. He mentions in the Preface of this collection that "I don't know why do I compose poetry? Yes, one thing I know for sure that whenever I become a victim of casteism, exploitation and oppression or whenever I see someone being victimised, something gets boiled up in me, which I attempt to capture in words (through poems)."[25]

In the title poem, *Suno Brahaman*, Malkhan Singh has not only questioned social structures but also revolted against it and asked directly the very *raison-de-tre* for caste system and its continuance. He writes:

(1)

The journey of our slavery
Begins from your birth
and it would end
with your end

(2)

Listen Brahaman
Our sweats
Stink to you
Then do one thing some day
Send your women
With our women
For sweeping (*maila kamane*)
And you!
Come with me
We would do
Leather work, jointly
Send your son with mine
In search of daily wage
And send your daughter
With ours to
To *Zamindars*' field for
Agricultural works
And tired by evening
Stretch over ground
Smell son, daughter and yourself
Only then you would know
The fragrance of life

That gets strengthened
Along with body odour

(3)

...do not forget
Labourers' shoulders
Are not ready to
Bear your burden
They are not ready at all.[26]
(*Suno Brahaman*)

This poem depicts anger of the *Dalit* community and resolves to fight against all kinds of exploitation and refuses to bear the burden of the upper castes. This also demands for equality (in terms of work and occupation) and narrates feelings in a striking style. The poem becomes representative of the feelings of the *Dalit* community when it asks for upper castes' women, sons and daughters to join hands with their lower castes counterparts and do the same work to understand the meaning of life and its struggle. This manifests level of anger as well as political articulation among *Dalits* who are not only being organised but also becoming politically conscious and vocal in assertion of their rights. In other poems, Malkhan has questioned caste as the sole identity of a human beings and rejects this category. He is also optimistic for future that things would change for *Dalits* and their continued struggle for equality and dignity would decisively prove fruitful to them.

Joothan (1997, Autobiography): Om Prakash Balmiki

Joothan: *Atma Katha* is the second autobiography in Hindi *Dalit* Literature, written by Om Prakash Balmiki, which got published in 1997. In the Preface, writer explains about his purpose and feelings to write an autobiography. He said, "The pains of *Dalit* life are intolerable and difficult to experience. These experiences have got no place in literary expressions. We have breathed in such social order that is very cruel and inhuman and is also insensitive towards the *Dalits*."[27]

Om Prakash Balmiki attempted many times to write his experiences but could not succeed. Later on, he wrote an autobiographical note for an edited book *'Harijan Se Dalit'* on the request of its editor, Raj Kishore. Subsequently, he decided to write down his experiences completely that came out as *Joothan*. Om Prakash Balmiki found "there were several dangers (*khateray*) in writing these experiences. I started writing in a systematic way after a long period of struggle within. This led me to relive atrocities, exploitation and deprivation. In this process, I experienced tremendous mental torture. I felt how painful it is to unlayer myself. Some people consider it unbelievable and exaggerated...but why should there be any doubt to pen down what is truth?"[28] Thus, *Joothan* is a narration of one's own life and its struggle depicting what it means to be a member of the *Dalit* community, what is the level of exploitation, discrimination and how difficult is the struggle for equality and dignity.

Joothan is an example of the *Dalit* protest literature and written "with anguish and a controlled anger agains: society"[29] as viewed by Sudha Pai. She writes, "The writer describes his childhood in a small village in Muzzafarnagar district, the struggle by his family to eke out a living, provide him and education and the ill-treatment by the local backward caste groups: the *Tyagis*. Constantly harassed and teased in the school by his classmates and his teachers, Om Prakash managed to gain an education and a government job. Written with anguish and a controlled anger against society, the book exhorts *Dalits* to improve their situation through education and critiques society for ill treatment and marginalisation of *Dalits*, particularly the *Balmiki* sub-caste to which he belongs as sweepers and cleaners."[30] We would analyse *Joothan* with two sub-categories: socio-political context and struggle for identity and dignity.

Socio-political Context

Born in Muzaffarnagar district in western Uttar Pradesh, author spent his childhood "in an atmosphere characterised by stuffed narrow streets, pigs, half-naked children, dogs, daily quarrels"[31] along with acute poverty. The time period is early 1950s when he experienced untouchability in/around his surroundings, and with great much difficulty got admission in the school. From here starts his struggling journey for recognition and identity. In school he is exploited by teachers and was forced to clean school ground that barred him from attending the classes. In this context, author has mentioned his father's protest, who not only protested against this exploitation but also psychologically strengthened him, which had ever-lasting influence on the personality development of the author. Author is deeply influenced by his father who had always encouraged him to study. His father used to say that *"pad likh ke jaati sudharni hai"*[32] (you have to do a lot for the community after getting educated). His father also stopped the practice of *salaam* (in which newly wed couple from lower castes make a round of each house where their families are working and pay respect to them. In return, they get some donation from the upper castes). Author found this practice "most humiliating"[33] and considers it as "the height of caste pride and supremacy...this is a conspiracy to trap (lower castes) and humiliate them."[34] His father was very happy to note that his son has started questioning all these humiliating practices and customs prevalent in society, supported him to challenge those customs, and started breaking them in their personal life.

People from his community were doing all kinds of labour work for *Tyagis* right from harvesting to looking after their animals (cows, buffalo). In return, they were not only underpaid but were forced to do *Begar* also. Level of economic exploitation was very high and clubbed with social discrimination, this become the worst living atmosphere for the *Balmiki* community. Mentioning the practice of *Joothan*,[35] author has referred to a very sensitive instance where his mother revolted against ill treatment and humiliation meted to them during one marriage in the village. Her vocal protest, subsequently, put an end to this practice in his house.

Author got exposed to literature roughly when he was in standard VIII. He read Sarat Chandra, Premchand, Rabindranath Tagore and got influenced by their writings. Later on, this provided him an opportunity to critically examine literary trends and aesthetics prevalent in Hindi literature. For him, "Hell is just an imagination in literature. But for us life is no less than hell, particularly during rainy season. We have experienced hell in its personified form. These painful and torturous experiences have not reached the great poets of Hindi. How horrible is this reality."[36] He further noticed literature, especially poetry as "very much artificial and false devoid of grassroots realities of rural society."[37] Then, he started writing poems, which challenged *Brahmanism*, caste oppression and exploitation.

Om Prakash Balmiki passed Secondary examinations and became the first one from his community to do so. His father celebrated his success and he got encouragement from one *Tyagi* named Chaman Lal *Tyagi*. This was an unusual event during those days that "made him emotional, because this kind of behaviour was never expected amidst rampant exploitation and humiliation."[38]

These are some of the instances, which indicate oppressive social structure, caste oppression, economic exploitation, social discrimination and humiliation. This social context makes the author to question Hindu Caste Society and subsequently challenging it in all possible ways. He failed in the Intermediate examination despite securing good marks in all subjects except Chemistry practical papers (in fact, he was not allowed to do experiments in the lab on one or other pretext by his teacher). This led him to shift to Dehradun where he got admitted in DAV Inter College. Here he got an opportunity to know and read about Dr. Ambedkar that facilitated him to articulate his anger. He got a direction after reading about Dr. Ambedkar as he acknowledged in the following lines: "A live consciousness generated within me after reading these books (on the life and works of Dr. Ambedkar). These books gave words to my numbness. The feeling of protest against system strengthened within me during these days... A new word *Dalit* was also added in my vocabulary, which was not replacement for the term *'Harijan'* but expression of anger of millions of untouchables... I got a new direction... My anger started articulating... literature provided me this courage."[39]

Then he got job as an apprentice in the Ordinance Factory, Dehradun and after completing training was selected for further training at Jabalpur in Madhya Pradesh. "This opened the new avenues of 'progress' for him."[40] From here onwards, we notice a different person who subsequently became an activist for the *Dalit* empowerment and emancipation. Now we would discuss this phase as continuation of struggle for identity and dignity.

His days in Jabalpur were the days of personality development for him. He got exposed to Marxist ideology and literature, read Maxim Gorky's *Mother* and several stories by Chekhov. He also started participating in a Theatre Group and acted in numerous plays. Active participation in literary and cultural activities developed a new perspective towards literature as well as life. Then he appeared in the interview for Ordinance Factory Training Institute, Ambernath (Bombay) and got selected. He utilised this opportunity also to read world literature (like the works of Victor Hugo, Tolstoy Romain Rolland and many more).

Days in Bombay provided him an opportunity to know about the Marathi *Dalit* Literature, the *Dalit* Panther and the *Dalit* activism. He started active participation and formed a theatre group, *Meghdoot Natya Samstha.* This group became famous for its progressive commitment, and performed street and stage plays, organised exhibitions and several progressive events under the active leadership of the author.

His socialisation and politicisation got him associated with the contemporary *Dalit* movement. His involvement in the *Dalit* movement proved to be "self-satisfactory and a new experience"[41] for him, where he was able to contribute through his writings and activism challenging caste oppression and at the same time organising community for protest against exploitation. He has been the witness of Name Changing Movement of *Marathwada* University that had great impact on the *Dalits* and their struggle for dignity. He has also been witness to the politics of the Republican Party of India and the *Dalit* Panthers' Movement. These activities formed his political perspective and he made literature his weapon to fight against exploitation and discrimination. He has also actively participated in several political struggles for equality and dignity. He has noticed that discrimination is rampant in almost every aspect of life and it is very, very difficult for a member of the *Dalit* community to achieve 'success' in society. He experienced discrimination and humiliation right from his childhood and his consistent struggle made him a conscious political being who challenges exploitation and discrimination wherever it persists. He has contributed, like many other *Dalit* litterateurs, to the *Dalit* movement through his progressive and powerful writings, which demand for redefinitions of almost every component of social structure and its philosophical justifications.

Towards the end of his autobiography, Om Prakash Balmiki raised several pertinent questions and asked for redefinitions of socio-eco-political structures of the Indian society. He writes, "Caste is an important component in Indian society. Caste determines everything from the time of one's birth. Birth is not in the hand or a choice of a person. If I could be so, why I would have born in a sweepers' family? Those who call themselves as the custodians of the great cultural traditions of this country are born with their choice? But they take help of several scriptures to justify their birth. These religious scriptures do not advocate equality and independence but establish feudal mindsets."[42]

He further noticed, "Time has changed. But there is something, which is not making us comfortable. Many people attempted to know why there is hatred in the minds of upper castes towards the *Dalits*? Why plants and birds (animism) worshipping Hindu is so intolerant towards the *Dalits*? Today caste is a distinct and important component. Everything remains fine unless your caste status is unknown, but every thing changes the moment it becomes clear. The pain of being a *Dalit* circulates through veins like the edge of a knife. How the elite upper caste Hindus will come to know the pain of being a *Dalit*, of poverty, illiteracy, diliapated life conditions and much more?"[43]

Om Prakash Balmiki asked, "Why caste should be my identity? Some friends indicate towards the loud and arrogant writings. They indicate that I have a narrow vision. Literary expression should be articulated in a broader sense. One should come out of narrowness. Means my being a *Dalit* and my perspective complimenting to my socio-economic conditions and atmosphere indicates becomes arrogance for them." He further found the reason for such indication that "it is because I am, in their views, only an SC (Scheduled Caste), standing outside their door."[44]

Thus we find that *Joothan* is an autobiography of a person who has been subject to multiple oppressions, repeated harassment and humiliation. The author develops his own political understanding, participated in the *Dalit* movement and contributed through his writings, which substantially forms protest literature.

Many critics have commended Om Prakash Balmiki's effort to bring to notice his struggle, which is representative of larger struggle of the *Dalits* in the country for equality, dignity and solidarity. Kanwal Bharati considers it as an "epic"[45] against the system that "forms heaven for the upper castes and hell for the *Dalits*."[46] These initial two autobiographies (*Apne Apne Pinjare* and *Joothan*) started new trends in the Hindi *Dalit* Literature and many *Dalit* writers wrote their autobiographical accounts either in the form of an autobiographical note or a series in different literary magazines. For example "excerpts from Dr. Shyoraj Singh *'Bechain*'s autobiography titled Asthiyon Ke Akshar published in *Hans*, R.N. Sagar's autobiography titled, Jab Mujhe Chor Kaha and Jai Prakash Kardam's Meri Jaat."[47] In this way, we notice that *Joothan* has contributed immensely for the consolidation of the Hindi *Dalit* Literature.

Gunga Nahin Tha Main (1997, Poetry): Jai Prakash Kardam

Gunga Nahin Tha Main is a collection of twenty-five poems composed by Jai Prakash Kardam that got published in 1997. In Preface to this collection, Jai Prakash writes, "this is correct that the *Dalit* literature is a literature of rejection (*nakaar*). But this is the rejection of those systems, beliefs and traditions, which are irrational and useless for the society and the nation. Since these are useless they have no value. Equality, Independence and Fraternity are the most precious values for any society and nation and the *Dalit* Literature accepts these values as its core values."[48]

He composed poems with this understanding and came out with this collection. Pointing out level of discrimination and atrocities, he writes the title poem, *Gunga Nahin Tha Main* that reveals how upper castes students lobby against the lower castes students and on protest this could lead to violent encounters with them hampering their studies and subsequently rustication of the lower castes students from the school.

In another poem, Ambedkar Ki Santan, Jai Prakash pointed out towards protest and movement led by the *Dalits*, as he writes:

> ...Children of Ambedkar
> would not tolerate anymore
> Exploitation and Atrocities
> would not remain silent; would ask for all accounts
> for tears of Krishna; helpless of *Harkhu* and mourning of *Hariya*

and would break chains of injustice and exploitation
To write a new history[49]
In the same way, he asked for equality in all walks of life and writes:
...this will not continue now
there has to be
Equality in all spheres of life
right from governance to administration
from the works of sweeping and cleaning
to leather works
Equality has to be ensured[50]

Thus we find that there is an increased level of consciousness among the *Dalit* writers in Hindi Literature who are not only questioning exploitative social system but also encouraging people to get organised in this struggle. Here it is important to note that literary expression is being utilised as a weapon in this movement for equality and dignity, thus making the Hindi *Dalit* Literature as political literature that protests against exploitation.

Harry Kab Aayega (1999, Short Stories): Suraj Pal Chauhan

Harry Kab Aayega is a short stories collection by Suraj Pal Chauhan that got published in 1999. These short stories are representative of the *Dalit* community "that has been marginalized for centuries."[51] In the Preface, Suraj Pal Chauhan writes, "the feelings of the so called upper castes were always taken care of but it seems that the feelings of a very large section of society, *i.e.*, *Dalits* have been deliberately ignored. Now when the *Dalits* themselves are able to articulate their expression, it should be welcomed by all."[52] Further, he raised hopes that his short stories would generate introspection among the upper castes also.

The short stories, interestingly, are preceded by two write-ups: one is the Introductory titled 'Stories Churning Social Consciousness' by Jai Prakash Kardam and the other is a Reader's Perspective by Pramod Singh. Furthermore, the collection is dedicated to Om Prakash Balmiki and to the characters of these stories. Here it is to be noted that the initiatives taken by Mohan Dass Naimishray and Om Prakash

Balmiki had immense impact on the contemporary *Dalit* writers in Hindi Literature and in the process, they started articulating their anger against the system as well their vision for a new society.

These stories represent consistent struggle by the *Dalits* as is noticed by Jai Prakash Kardam in his Introductory. He found that "stories by Suraj Pal Chauhan are influenced by Dr. Ambedkar, who said–tolerating injustice is encouraging it."[53] Thus, his characters are not ready to tolerate injustice and exploitation. There is resistance to exploitation. For instance, in story titled, Parivartan Ki Baat the lower castes (*Chamars*) refused to remove a dead cow, a job assigned to their castes for nothing. They jointly refused such job despite all pressures from the upper castes (*Thakurs*). They were ready to pay any price for such a decision because they consider this job not only as forced one but also as humiliating. Another story Angoori symbolises a *Dalit* woman's courage and struggle for dignity, when two upper castes men attempted to physically assault her, she resisted their assault and her courageous resistance forced men to run away from her house. In this way, these stories portray in a very sensitive manner and simple communicative narration, utter level of discrimination and exploitation in different spheres of life that a *Dalit* lives.

Pramod Singh in his comment found that "these stories are successful in exposing upper castes' mindsets, conspiracy against the *Dalits* and justifications for the caste system."[54] Other critics have also appreciated this collection. Mohan Dass Naimishray commented "in almost every story, there is a clear expression of change and consciousness, which is also the aim of the *Dalit* Literature. The characters of his stories are not only poor and helpless, as we find in Premchand and other upper caste writers, but they have self-respect and will power that make them successful to break the vicious cycle of *Mannuvadi* mindsets."[55] In this way, we find that this collection proves to be an important contribution in the Hindi *Dalit* Literature, articulating not only anger but also a vision for equality, dignity and solidarity. This also has influenced successive *Dalit* writers in their literary expression and articulation.

After analysing these primary texts from the Hindi *Dalit* Literature, it is evident that there exists strong and emerging *Dalit* Literature in Hindi that is challenging Hindu Caste System in all walks of life. In addition, it is also questioning the very concept of literary expression and its aesthetic perspective: whether, it should depict the reality as it exists and being experienced or it should be portrayed with linguistic sophistication and 'polished' expression. In this regard, there are several literary magazines, which exclusively focus on *Dalit* issues and attempt to generate political consciousness among the community. For example, Jai Prakash Kardam is editing *Dalits Sahitya: An Annual Edition of Dalits Literature and Culture*[56] and has come out with four volumes since 1999. This is an attempt to bring divergent perspectives on the *Dalit* movement, literature and life. Another magazine is *Yudhrat Aam Aadami* a quarterly coming from Bihar/ Jharkhand. It is to be noted that a serious efforts are being put in to bring out such collections and these efforts are facilitating consolidation of the *Dalit* identity through literary-political mobilisation that, in turn, is embedded in the contemporary *Dalit* assertion in northern part of India.

NOTES

1. Pai, Sudha. *Ibid.*
2. Naimishray, Mohandas. *Apne Apne Pinjare* (Delhi: Vaani Prakashan, 1995), p. 11.
3. *Ibid.* p. 17.
4. *Ibid.* p. 18.
5. Nagar, Amrit Lal. *Ibid.* p. 343.
6. Naimishray, Mohandas. *Ibid.* p. 18.
7. *Ibid.* p. 44-51.
8. *Ibid.* p. 40.
9. *Ibid.* p. 27.
10. *Ibid.* p. 107.
11. *Ibid.* p. 107.
12. *Ibid.* p. 32.
13. *Ibid.* p. 57.
14. *Ibid.* p. 39.
15. *Ibid.* p. 74.
16. *Ibid.* p. 75.
17. *Ibid.* p. 136.
18. *Ibid.* Dedication page.
19. Kumar, Abhay. *Dalit Atmakatha Ki Parampara aur Apne Apne Pinjare* (excerpts from unpublished M. Phil. Dissertation in the Centre of Indian

Languages, School of Language, Literature and Culture Studies, Jawaharlal Nehru University Delhi, 1998).

20. Meenu, Rajat Rani. *Atmakatha Ki Parampara aur Dalit Atmakathaye* in Shyoraj Singh *'Bechain'* and Devendra Chaube (ed.) *Ibid.* p. 161.
21. Marmat, Avantika Prasad. *Kranti Shesh Hai: Kavya Sankalan* (Ujjan: Madhya Pradesh *Dalit* Sahitya Academy, 1995) Note before poems.
22. *'Rahi'*, Lalchand. *Kranti Shesh Hai: Kavya Sankalan* (Ujjan: Madhya Pradesh *Dalit* Sahitya Academy, 1995) p. 9.
23. *Ibid.* p. 21.
24. *Ibid.* p. 6.
25. Singh, Malkhan. *Suno Brahaman* (Rampur: Bodhisatva Prakashan, 1996) Preface.
26. *Ibid.* p. 45-8.
27. Balmiki, Om Prakash. *Joothan* (Delhi: Radha Krishna Prakashan, 1997) p. 7.
28. *Ibid.* p. 8.
29. Pai, Sudha. *Ibid.*
30. *Ibid.*
31. Balmiki, Om Prakash. *Ibid.* p. 11.
32. *Ibid.* p. 40.
33. *Ibid.* p. 45.
34. *Ibid.* p. 45.
35. *Ibid.* 20-1.
36. *Ibid.* 35.
37. *Ibid.* 51.
38. *Ibid.* 75.
39. *Ibid.* 89.
40. *Ibid.* 99.
41. *Ibid.* 121.
42. *Ibid.* 159-60.
43. *Ibid.*160.
44. *Ibid.* 160.
45. Quoted in Rajat Rani 'Meenu'. *Ibid.* p. 162.
46. *Ibid.*p. 162.
47. *Ibid.* p. 167.
48. Kardam, Jai Prakash. *Gunga Nahin Tha Main* (Delhi: Atish Prakashan, 1997) p. 7.
49. *Ibid.* 49-51.
50. *Ibid.* 16.
51. Chauhan, Suraj Pal. *Harry Kab Aayega* (Ghaziabad: Anubhav Prakashan, 1999) Preface.
52. *Ibid.*
53. *Ibid.* p. 6.
54. *Ibid.* p. 12.
55. *Ibid.* On front flap of the book.
56. Kardam, Jai Prakash (ed.) Dalit Sahitya 1999 to 2002 (Delhi).

6

Dalit Politics and Literature

Future Trends

The last quarter of the Twentieth Century reflected tremendous changes in the Indian Political System and represented political assertions by new social forces. We have analysed, in the last chapter, the progressive direction of the *Dalit* movement in the country that started with the struggle for recognition of the human personality and moved towards actual sharing of power in the Indian democracy. We have also analysed the impact of the Ambedkar that, not only consolidated political consciousness among the *Dalits* but also, guided the very course of the *Dalit* movement in India. It is important to observe that in northern part of the country, influence of the Ambedkarite movement was felt roughly during the time of Independence, which advocated the *Dalit* question on political lines rather than on any moral grounds.

In northern India, the *Dalit* movement was also limited to certain pockets and we also noted absence of any major anti-caste social movement in the region. To understand level of political consciousness and participation of the *Dalits*, we also analysed thoroughly the origin, nature and strength of the *Dalit* movement and found that there was much influence of Mahatma Gandhi upon the anti-colonial struggle in the northern region, that shaped the identity of the *Dalits* and made problems of 'Untouchability' as a moralistic rather than political one. But it also to be noted that a small section of the community rejected Gandhian view under the influence of Dr. Ambedkar towards the end of the colonial period and began to use politics as a means to achieve an equal status in the Indian polity. Since Independence, *Dalit* movement has passed through a number of phases of strengths and weaknesses, autonomy and co-optation has and carved out its own political space with the larger political framework of the region. The Republican Party of India (RPI) in the 1960s raised some hopes for independent *Dalit* assertion but proved to be short lived due to lack of dynamic leadership, internal divisions over the strategy for the struggle and the ability of the Congress to consolidate the majority of the *Dalits* within its fold. But the formation of the Bahujan Samaj Party (BSP) gave a new impetus to the movement and succeeded in breaking down the vertical patron-client relationship with the upper castes and accompanying political mobilisation pattern of the vote banks which was characteristic of one of the largest states with substantial proportion of the *Dalit* population: Uttar Pradesh, for a long time has constructed new mobilisational solidarities on horizontal dimensions. Remarkably, political programmes and ideological perspectives of the BSP are vague in nature though it has been successful in capturing political power and infused confidence among the *Dalits* for further consolidation and assertion for political identity. In this way, the BSP seeks to be both a movement and political party with a short-term goal of capturing political power and a long-term aim of social transformation.

Since mid-1980s, we find an overall challenge that is being given to the upper castes' hegemony by the *Dalits* in every field: political, intellectual, cultural and many more. In this regard, A. Gajendran notes that "when one explores the historicity of *Dalits*, their ethno-linguistic heterogeneity is manifested in all their socio-cultural features-festivals, religion, music, dance, food habits, medicine system and so on. However, a point to be noted is that traditionally many *Dalit* communities seem to have accepted Buddhist values and incorporated them in their respective regional cultural features, thereby challenging the conventional understanding of a homogenised process which uprooted all *Dalit* communities from their cultural milieu and accommodated them within a sub-continental boundary called Hindu India."[1] Accordingly, there is a process of challenging mainstream hegemony by the oppressed and disadvantaged section of the Indian society at every possible level and this challenge is a result of a long-drawn *Dalit* movement in the course of the history of the last century. There have been several studies on the roots of the *Dalit* consciousness during the recent past, for instance, Eleanor Zelliot traces the roots of the *Dalit* consciousness, "which allow pride, self-respect and a vision of the future...in the older movements of the *Adi-Dharm* of Punjab and Uttar Pradesh, the Satnami of Chhatisgarh, the Narayana Guru movement in Kerala and in the contemporary period the *Dalit* movement in Karnataka, the rise of a *Dalit* Christian movement in Tamil Nadu and Andhra Pradesh, the phenomenon of Kanshi Ram, Mayawati and the BSP in Uttar Pradesh, the new political thrust in Tamil Nadu and, of course, the *Dalits* of Maharasthtra with their ever more creative forays into the modern world of education and culture."[2]

We have also discussed in the last chapters, particularly in Chapter three and four, how political consciousness among the *Dalits* in northern belt progressed on the lines of mobilisation, strategies, politics and identity. It is noticeable in this regard that during 1930s the *Dalit* question in this region was understood as a 'moral' one and we find its reflection in the creative literature also (for example, works of Premchand) where transformation of heart of the uppers castes was considered as a pertinent solution to this problem. Subsequently, as the political dynamics of the regions get changed, we noticed change of literary syntax, both in terms of form and content. Thus, it could be said that level of political consciousness among the *Dalits* facilitated literary expression of the Hindi *Dalit* Literature that portrayed *Dalit* politics and its issues of self-dignity and identity completely from a different perspectives. We find obvious parallels to the political trends in literary expression and contemporary Hindi *Dalit* Literature which has opened new vistas for reinterpretation of earlier works by the upper castes on the life of the *Dalit* community and also makes an attempt to establish their own aesthetic notions of literary expression. In this regard, we would discuss some of the views on theories of the *Dalit* aesthetics, but before coming to that issue, it is pertinent to analyse some of the recent political trends in contemporary *Dalit* politics in the country.

It has been discussed earlier in this study that the *Dalit* movement in the northern region started as a reformative movement that attempted to purify Hinduism of its evils, and fought against the tyranny of the Caste System. Egalitarian preaching of the saints like Kabir, Ravidas and other shaped *Dalit* consciousness during this period and played important role in the awakening of *Dalit* consciousness. There were also attempts for internal reformation within the community and with proliferation of the Ambedkar movement emphasis was given for new self-image and identity based on education, political mobilisation and assertion. There were numerous problems faced by the Movement, for instance, weaker organizational strength and financial resources, but with the unleashing of new mobilisational plank, the community asserted with great political force that was largely consolidated by the BSP. Further, it has also been observed that rejection of *Brahminism* and Hinduism became important political component for the sustenance of the movement. In this direction, Dr. Ambedkar embraced Buddhism to build an alternative, equitable and egalitarian society and became the torchbearer for posterity.

Coming to the contemporary *Dalit* discourse, we find that *Dalit* politics has carved out its independent political space and is endeavouring to consolidate its assertion in different parts of the region. Underlining the quest for identity remains most important issue along with several others for the *Dalit* discourse, as has been observed by Ghanshyam Shah, "there has not been a single, unified *Dalit* movement in the country, now or in the past. Different movements have highlighted different issues related to *Dalits*, around different ideologies. However, all of them, overtly or covertly, assert a *Dalit* identity, though its meaning is not identical and precise for everyone. Identity is concerned with the self-esteem and self-image of a community-real or imaginary-dealing with the existence and role: 'Who are WE?' 'What position do we have in society *vis-à-vis* other communities?' 'How are we related to others?' Notwithstanding differences in the nature of *Dalit* movements and the meaning of identity, there has been a common quest-the quest for equality, self-dignity and eradication of untouchablity."[3] Here, it is to be recalled that level of political consciousness performs the task of 'a functional catalyst' for shaping identity among the *Dalits*, particularly its subjective understanding of the self and objective cognition of the socio-eco-politico-cultural conditions. We have already discussed catalyst role played by the political consciousness in chapter three of this study. Hence, question of identity becomes central to the *Dalit* discourse, which means a dignified human life with equality, liberty and solidarity as the cherished principles with a visionary transformation of society towards egalitarian social system.

In addition to identity building, the *Dalit* discourse is also making efforts to highlight caste based discrimination at different international forums like the United Conference against Racism, Racial Discrimination, Xenophobia and Related Intolerance held at Durban during 27 August to 7 September 2001. This Conference was used as a forum to bring to notice the prevalent social discrimination based on caste status to the international community and at the same time, provided an opportunity to debate this issue afresh internally by different developmental actors of the civil society in India. The official position of the Government of India "was marked by an effort to keep discussions related to caste and caste based discrimination out of the inter-governmental forum"[4] but it becomes pertinent due to the efforts made by many *Dalit* and human rights activists to restart an internal debate on the issue of race, caste and caste based discrimination. There was an attempt through the participation in the Durban process with the "hope that concerted external pressure would impel the Indian state into more effective implementation of the existing laws and schemes as also radically reform the social space to usher in genuine equality as citizens...and all these have once again brought the *Dalit* question to the fore. Whatever our position on the academic or political implications or caste and race, or of the emergence of new forums and new actors using new language and strategies, the longstanding questions of exclusion, discrimination and oppression based on caste remain."[5]

The Durban process also brought to the notice the issue of entitlement that who is entitled to talk about the *Dalits* both at the national and international level? We have already discussed this issue while analysing the course of the *Dalit* movement (Gandhi-Ambedkar divide) and also development of the Hindi *Dalit* Literature (who would write literature on the *Dalit* issues?). Here also we find a close relationship between literary expression and political discourse. That *Dalits* themselves enjoy the natural right to speak on the issues concerning their lives is being critically advocated by *Dalit* litterateurs and much vehemently during the recent past. In this regard, Gopal Guru argued that "the *Dalits* claim for being legitimate representatives of their issues, including at Durban, can be justified on the grounds that it is they who took the initiative to bring caste into forefront of the public domain, however elitist and limited the framework of this domain may be. Thus, at an epistemic level, privileging the *Dalit* voice on the *Dalit* question can be justified. Second, the representation of *Dalits* by non-*Dalits* becomes problematic since it accords to the claimant a kind of morally superior position without realising that it sustains itself on the basis of a permanent exclusion of *Dalits* from the intellectual domain. It reproduces new forms of intellectual hierarchy, thus making difficult the democratisation of intellectual representation. It marks the continuation of *Dalit* submergence into the language of the alien. It is primarily in this sense that a *Dalit* speaking for the *Dalits* can be justified; it helps the historical recovery of the *Dalit* voice."[6] It is being observed that active participation in the Durban process is the result of increased level of political consciousness among *Dalits* forcing people from almost all walks of life to pay serious attention to their issues and working together for accomplishment of liberty, equality and solidarity for the upliftment of the *Dalits* and oppressed.

Another significant event that happened in the *Dalit* discourse having impact on the very expression of political consciousness among the *Dalits* is the Bhopal Conference: 'Charting A New Course for *Dalits* For the 21st Century' held at Bhopal on 12-13 January 2002. The Conference, attended by many intellectuals and activists, deliberated "the issues concerning the welfare of and justice to the 250 million *Dalits*".[7] Declaring belief in Dr. Ambedkar's ideal for social democracy and endorsing "the ideals of civil society enshrined in the Constitution of India, particularly its Preamble that declares the Indian State's commitment to Justice, Liberty, Equality and Fraternity"[8] the Conference recognised "that for *Dalits* to make common cause with other liberation and human rights movements in and outside the country."[9] The Conference adopted a visionary 21 Point Action Agenda for the 21st Century that addresses each and every aspect of the life of the *Dalits* very comprehensively and demands for concerted efforts and positive contribution by all for equal opportunity, democratisation and civil society. It would be pertinent to mention 21 Point Action Agenda[10] here that would provide a comprehensive view of the major issues in the contemporary *Dalit* discourse:

1. Ensure that each *Dalit* family will own enough cultivable

land for socio-economic well-being. The government should pursue all possible measures including the distribution of surplus land, government revenue lands and temple lands within a specific timeframe. If the need be, the government should purchase cultivable land and distribute it among *Dalits*.

2. Enact legislation and enforce it stringently to enable *Dalits* to have an equitable share in the appropriation and use of the rural and urban common property resources. The law must be amended to ensure that lengthy litigation, with the ulterior motive of denying *Dalits* of legal redressal, is not resorted to.
3. Enact legislation and enforce the right of *Dalit* agricultural labourers to living wages, to gender parity in wages, to job security, to better working conditions and welfare measures, and to ensure punitive measures against offenders.
4. Appoint Statutory Committees at the national and state level to identify within specified timeframe all the *Dalits* lands occupied by non-*Dalits*, to assess the quantum of compensation to be paid by non-*Dalits* for their illegal utilisation of lands, to identify the original owners and their nearest kith and kin for restoring these lands back to them, to expedite legal proceedings in courts specially appointed for this purpose against the illegal occupants and to ensure punitive measures against them.
5. Ensure the restoration of the alienated lands to the tribals, restore their rights over forest and forest-produce, provide them with compensation and rehabilitation measures, extend resources and capacity building measures for gainful utilisation of their lands and forests and make those *Dalits* displaced due to construction of dams/developmental projects and mining as shareholders of such enterprises.
6. Democratise Capital so as to ensure proportionate share for SCs and STs. Make budgetary allocation for SC and STs to enable them enter the market economy with adequate investment resources, and develop their capacities and skills for such market enterprises.
7. Enforce with stringent measures the Bonded Labour System (Abolition) Act, 1976 and abolish forthwith child labour to

ensure freedom with dignity for all *Dalits*, and accordingly make suitable amendments in the appropriate legislations.

8. Amend Art. 21 of the Constitution of India so as to include the following rights for all citizens, with special emphasis on SCs and STs, and on the basis of two criteria: namely, low-economic income and without religious discrimination: the rights to a standard of living adequate for the health and well-being of women and men equally, including food, safe drinking water, clothing, housing, public health and medical care, social security and social services; the right to living wage and the right to own 5 acres of cultivable land or to gainful employment.
9. Implement compulsory, free and high quality education for all *Dalits* immediately, make allocation of funds proportionate to their number and level of the illiterates, ensure compensation to those families which forfeit their income from child-labour, increase the number and amount of scholarships, and provide better infrastructural facilities in SC and AT schools and offer market-oriented vocational and technical education.
10. Make the reservation quota applicable in all the public and private educational institutions from primary to technical and professional levels. Every SC/ST child with low income-base must be given quality free-education at the State's expense. And every English medium school must implement 'Diversity in Admissions'.
11. Recognise SC and ST women as a distinct category among women, and accordingly make segregated data on *Dalit* women available in census reports, action taken reports and progress reports, evolve nation and state level perspective plans for mainstreaming SC and ST women in developmental programmes, market enterprises, financial allocation, reservation facilities in education, employment and health facilities, and mandate the National and State Commissions for SCs and STs for Women to study and report specifically the status of SC and ST Women in their annual reports.
12. Implement effectively, in letter and spirit, the SC and ST (Prevention of Atrocities) Act, 1989 and Rules, 1995,

especially with regard to atrocities against *Dalit* women, and accordingly prosecute the dominate caste leaders and their unions who stoke the fire of caste clashes and the police officials acting in connivance with them. In cases of atrocities against SC/STs, a system of collective punishment has to be evolved as oppressors enjoy community's support and protection and escapes the law.

13. Ensure Diversity or SC/STs' due representation in all public institutions of India, whether universities of academic or autonomous or registered bodies. Those institutions, which do not abide by the principle of *Affirmative Action*, must lose recognition and state funding. All private industry/ corporate houses must accept and implement 'Diversity in workforce' immediately.
14. Ensure that in all state and national budgets allocations are made as per the proportion of SC and ST population and penal action taken against unutilisation or diversion of funds meant for these sections.
15. Every government and private organisation must implement Supplier Diversity from socially disadvantaged businesses and Dealership Diversity in all goods and services.
16. The State must assume sole responsibility in protecting the SCs and STs. The State must identify those atrocity-prone areas and deploy forces. In addition, provide arms licences to the SCs and STs as stipulated in the Atrocities Act for self-defence purpose, make the setting up of *Dalit* self-defence groups from village onwards mandatory, and specially train *Dalit* women to handle weapons in self-defence against the perpetrators of crimes and atrocities.
17. Eliminate the humiliating practice of manual scavenging on an urgent footing through effective rehabilitation, alternative and sustainable employment measures and developmental programmes, and prosecute violators of the Employment of Manual Scavengers and Construction of Dry Latrines (Prohibition) Act, 1993, especially the gross violator- Railways, Defence, Urban Local Bodies and others.
18. Make it statutory for Parliament and state assemblies to debate on the annual reports of the national and state level

Commissions for SC/STs and *Safai Karamcharis* within the following year, and ensure that these annual reports and the action-taken reports are make public. And ensure that the action is taken under clear statutory stipulations.

19. Make affirmative action mandatory in all private institutions, including industries and corporate sectors, which receive State patronage in any form-from land at concessional rate to tax benefits etc. and also develop the capacities and skills of *Dalits* to help them meet the demands of these different sectors.
20. Implement the policy of reservation to SC/STs at all levels of Judiciary and defence forces. And make transparent appointment process in Judiciary by doing away with the nomination system.
21. Bring out a Truth Paper in two years on the status of reservation during the past 25 years and place it before Parliament and state assemblies for debate, and on a war-footing fill immediately all the backlog posts meant for *Dalits* and that, too, only with *Dalit* candidates.

Thus, we find that the Bhopal Declaration addressed each and every issue concerning the welfare of the *Dalits* in India right from the land reforms, common property rights, right to work, democratisation of capital in the market economy, implementation of reservation policies at all levels of administration and governance, women's empowerment to right to a standard of living with dignified human existence. This Declaration manifests high level of political consciousness among the *Dalits*, who are challenging discrimination in all spheres amidst globalisation and liberalisation of Indian economy.

It is to be noted with serious attention that this Declaration is not restricted to demand justice, equality and freedom in the government offices but also addresses private and market institutions, making it evident that equality only in the government offices and that too of a very formal nature would not curb/ eliminate social and economic discrimination that is prevalent in all walks of life in our society. Hence, it demands effective implementation of the existing, statutes, Acts, policies and rules and also evolution of new systems for Diversity that could ensure maximum representation and participation of the *Dalits* and their contribution with democratic social transformation of society. Thus, it can be said that the Bhopal Declaration demands for democracy, decentralisation and transparency in the administration and governance of the country.

Coming to the literary expression of these trends, one finds numerous parallels in Hindi *Dalit* Literature, which are narrating these trends. We have discussed in the last chapter how issues of identity, mobilisation, land reforms, dignified human existence, women's issues and activism for social transformation for equal opportunities and democracy are being depicted in literary works. Here, it is pertinent to mention that recent works in literature, (largely from mid-1980s) particularly by Mohan Dass Naimishray, Om Prakash Balmiki, Suraj Pal Chauhan and others are portraying different aspects of the life of the *Dalits* and also resolved entitlement issue (Who would write *Dalit* Literature?) on political lines. These trends in Hindi *Dalit* Literature reflect enhanced level of political consciousness that works as a functional catalyst for the organisation and mobilisation of the *Dalits* to continue their movement.

Associated with the above observation, another significant issue needs to be discussed briefly so as to provide holistic picture of the contemporary *Dalit* politics and literature in Hindi. This is the issue of the evolution of aesthetics within Hindi *Dalit* Literature. We would very briefly elaborate on some of the views in this direction.

Kanwal Bharati[11] considers three major streams in Hindi *Dalit* Literature, *viz.*, first stream represents literature written by the *Dalits* themselves (which is experiential); second stream is of "the Hindu authors"[12] (for whom portrayal of *Dalits* is a matter of pleasure); and the third stream is that of the progressive writers (who view *Dalits* as proletariat). In his view, the *Dalit* literary discourse is guided by the Ambedkar movement and above two streams except the second one, are attempting to highlight trauma of the life of the *Dalits*. He also finds progressive writers' contribution very significant to the cause and further elaborates, "*Dalit* discourse in the contemporary *Dalit* Literature is representing social revolution and it has to move towards economic revolution. There has to be a convergence of social and economic revolution and only then the *Dalit* community in India would emerge as a strong political force".[13]

These remarks make it very clear that the Hindi *Dalit* Literature endeavours for social and economic revolution and these principles are becoming the very foundation of the new sense of aesthetics with this discourse. Based on these two principles as guiding force of the Ambedkar movement, the *Dalit* Literature envisions progressive and revolutionary transformation of society that could definitely ensure justice, equality, and liberty for all. In this way, aesthetic values of the Hindi *Dalit* Literature are political in nature and make this stream of literature the political one.

Sharan Kumar Limbale, who advocates sociological aesthetics of *Dalit* Literature, considered that "*Dalit* litterateurs have done objective and realistic critique of literature as well as make attempts to evolve sociological aesthetics…which means that *Dalit* authors have rejected conventional aesthetics carve independent space for their own sphere of aesthetics."[14] He raised a pertinent question as how convention/traditional sense of aesthetics (which is largely pleasure driven) is compatible with *Dalit* Literature and consciousness among *Dalits*, which is primarily "revolutionary mindset"?[15] Realising the need for autonomous and independent sense of aesthetics, Limbale further elaborated that it has be based on the principles of equality, independence, justice and fraternity, hence, changing traditional aesthetics, which stands rejected with the development of the *Dalit* Literature. It draws its inspiration from the preaching and works of Buddha, Ṛavidas, Mahatma Jotiba Phule, Dr. Ambedkar, Sri Narayana Guru, E.V. Periyar Swami Naikar and Swami Acchutanand. This repository of distinguished personalities enriches the *Dalit* Literature that inspires us for making attempts to change discriminatory social system.

Thus, political consciousness among the *Dalits* as expressed through the *Dalit* Literature becomes objective, realistic and progressive that analysed subjective understanding of the self, objective cognition of socio-politico-cultural conditions, relationship within community and *vis-à-vis* other communities and envisions transformation of society with a visionary movement. It also emphasises on the transmission of knowledge from one generation to the other so as to build capacities of the future generations for an exploitation of free society.

Therefore, we find that literary expression of political

consciousness among the *Dalits* has gradually evolved its autonomous political space and challenged upper castes' hegemony in all spheres of life: social, political, economic, cultural and literary. In fact, it is due to the political changes taking place at the grassroots level, which are making *Dalit* politics and literature progressive and literature becomes best tool for the expression of not only of the feelings, emotions, torture and exploitation but also empowers *Dalits* to rise against exploitation and contributing for the establishment of an equal and equalitarian society.

Understanding literary expression of political consciousness among the *Dalits* is a challenging, complex and interesting task. It becomes crucial factor to identify certain trends, which are getting paralleled with grassroots level political development occurring in the Hindi belt, so as to obtain a holistic picture of the *Dalit* politics and its expression through protest *Dalit* literature. Analysis of several interrelated and interconnected factors provides us an opportunity to understand the *Dalit* politics from multidimensional perspective: political, social, economic, cultural and literary. Critical analysis of some of the works of Hindi literature also makes it possible to comprehend trends in these levels of operational analysis of different socio-eco-politico-cultural categories.

This study, guided by the ecological model of research with inter-disciplinary approach for analysis makes an attempt to understand levels of political consciousness spread over a period of roughly more than seventy years and also at different sites: individual (self and collective), immediate context, formal and informal institutions of social structure, socio-political and cultural environment and state. This study, though not based on exclusively empirical methods, attempts to interpret above sites critically that could provide us insights into the *Dalit* politics, literature and their interplay. In this endeavour, this study efforts to be innovative and creative without compromising objectivity of the level of analysis. We have thoroughly discussed processes of formation of political consciousness among the *Dalits*, its consolidation and proliferation and derived some of the important trends, which affected the course of the *Dalit* movement in this region and also politically sharpen the *Dalit* assertion through mobilisation and identity building.

In this process, we interacted with challenging tasks of the very definition of political consciousness that could be manifested and interpreted (not only through empirical data) but also through literary expression resembling with the ground reality. It is this quest to find out factors responsible for the formation and expression of political consciousness that led us to define it as 'a functional catalyst' that performs the tasks of subjective understanding of the self, transmission of knowledge from one generation to another, objective cognition of the socio-eco-politico-cultural conditions, critical relationship with other communities and the structures of power and economic controls and transformation of society consciously with a visionary movement. This kind of role attributed to the concept of political consciousness also broadens the nature and scope of both theoretical and applied politics. This definition makes the concept comprehensive that encompasses almost every aspect of one's life cycle. This definitional perspective is very important and proved immensely helpful to analyse creative works of literature, which also attempts to represent a holistic view of the situation.

Secondly, this study also attempted to understand the meaning of literary expression and particularly the *Dalit* literary expression. It observed during the course of its analysis that literature is not a static collection of written expressions authored by a writer nor is it mere documentation. Rather it is always evolving and developing, keeping tune with the changing times. Literature and its concepts are deeply associated with the development and progress of society. It is basically the development of the heart of the people and a cherished asset and accumulation of the knowledge of a particular time period reflecting society in a miroristic way. Literature becomes a christened reflection of the feelings of the masses along with the social relation combining it with literary imagination of a writer. It is essentially expression of the reality of human life and great pieces of literature depict that reality with communicable and lucid language facilitating narrative with readers' aesthetic and literary sense having long lasting influence on the heart and mind of the readers. It possesses spirit of independence and essence of aesthetics leading towards the enlightenment of life whether expressed in essay, stories, poetry, novels and autobiographical forms. Literature explores, analyses, understands, investigates and examines several issues of our life and provides its critique. Literature is not just any expression but generates aesthetic sense, movements and strength; provides mental and spiritual solace; strengthens our determination to overcome difficulties; associates us with the larger social communities and motivates for cherished principles of liberty, equality and solidarity.

Several ideological debates related to the interaction between literature and politics like Idealism, Positivism, Structuralism, Sociological Literary Criticism and Marxist Literary Criticism were also dealt comprehensively so as to obtain a clear understanding of this relationship and subsequently exploring the possibility for a theoretical narrative on the interplay of politics and literature. It was observed that every school of the sociology of literature (except Idealist) recognises close relationship between politics and literature, of course, with their specialised qualifications like some stress on the form whereas other emphasise on the role of structure in creation of the literary texts.

This theoretical narrative facilitates this study to analyse eleven selected works of the Hindi Literature on life of the *Dalits*. It is important to note that this stream of the Hindi Literature (*Dalit* Literature) is representing real picture of the community, its trauma and struggle for social change. It was substantially recognised throughout the course of this study that the *Dalit* Literature is essentially protest literature that strongly opposes discrimination in any form and also attempts to generate new sense of literary aesthetics that have been transcended from a sophisticated perspective to a realistic one to demolish the supremacy of structured forms of literary aesthetics. We observed that the Hindi *Dalit* Literature is cultivating it own literary space with a very high level of thinking that possesses sense of the freedom, essence of realistic aesthetics highlighting the ground realities of the *Dalit* community.

Further, the study attempted to understand the meaning of the term *Dalit* consciousness and also traces a brief history of the *Dalit* movement in India. We observed that *Dalit* consciousness is inherently political consciousness that rejects Brahmanism, upper castes' dominance and revolted against exploitation and oppression. The *Dalit* consciousness "is a symbol of change and revolution"[16] and become 'a functional catalyst' for the establishment of an egalitarian society ensuring justice, freedom, equality and dignity for one and all. This study also observed that the *Dalit* movement drew inspiration from the life and works of Buddha, Kabir, Ravidas, Phule and Dr. Ambedkar and consolidated through progressive mobilisation and initiated process of identity building. It is to be noted that the *Dalit* movement in the Hindi belt was initially influenced by the Gandhian perspective rather than the Ambedkarite one and we find similar trends in literary expression of that period in the works of Premchand and others. But with increasing influence of Dr. Ambedkar's views on the *Dalit* empowerment and emancipation, there occurred changes in political as well as literary expression, for instance in the works of Mohan Dass Naimishray and Om Prakash Balmiki. Our study also reveals that the *Dalit* movement in the beginning was Reformatory in nature where attempts were made to purify Hinduism of its evils and fought against the tyranny of the Caste System but later on Alternative movements were also envisioned to create an alternative socio-cultural structure where each individual can enjoy respectfully a dignified life without any kind of discrimination.

The Hindi *Dalit* Literature becomes most important reference point for the analysis of these alternative trends that provides insights to observe whether the contemporary literary trends are in tune with the grassroot level struggles and perception held by the *Dalits*. Another significant observation throughout the course of the study is the deep-rooted influence of the Ambedkarite ideology, programmes and perspective that is shaping *Dalit* consciousness and influencing the process of identity building. The study also identified three phases[17] of the *Dalit* awakening *viz.* era of struggle for the recognition of human existence (1920-50), era of restructuring through social mobility and political participation (1950-1985) and era of actual sharing of power (1985 onwards). Comprehensive analysis of these phases as well as Dr. Ambedkar's contribution helped us to identify some of the trends of the *Dalit* movement in India. These are indicative trends of the proliferation of the movement, its consolidation and quest for equality, liberty and solidarity.

Critical analysis of selected works of Hindi Literature led us to investigate the socio-political contexts as represented in these works and also to understand the nature of representation of the *Dalits*. Eleven texts were analysed starting from *Godan* (Premchand) that was published in 1936 to *Harry Kab Aayega* (Suraj Pal Chauhan) published in 1999. The range of works facilitated us to understand and analyse political development of these years, which were, in fact, very crucial years for the *Dalit* movement. It provided an opportunity to understand the Gandhian and Ambedkarite influence on the course of the *Dalit* movement in Hindi belt and also the development of the Hindi literary tradition that subsequently demands for new sense of aesthetics for literature, particularly the Hindi *Dalit* Literature. It is evident that there exists strong and emerging *Dalit* Literature in Hindi that is challenging Hindu Caste System in all possible ways. In addition, it is also questioning the very concept of literary expression and its aesthetic perspective: whether it should depict the reality as it exists and being experienced or it should be portrayed with linguistic sophistication and 'polished' expression.

The study further reveals that the contemporary *Dalit* discourse asserts rights of the *Dalits* much more politically and in a very organised manner, though there are variations from region to region. There are constructive efforts to address caste-based discriminations at all levels and forums like the Durban and the Bhopal Conferences. The study also observed that issue of entitlement (who would write literature or represent on the *Dalit* issues) is also becoming important in political and literary expression. The debate continues over this issue but reiterates natural right of the *Dalits* to speak for/on themselves as "it helps the historical recovery of the *Dalit* voice".[17]

Further, the Bhopal Conference that "charted out a new course for *Dalits* for the 21st Century"[19] and adopted 21-point action agenda addressed each and every issue concerning the welfare of the *Dalits* in India right from the land reforms, common property rights, right to work, democratisation of capital in the market economy, implementation of reservation policies at all levels of administration and governance, women's empowerment to right to a standard of living with dignified human existence.

Thus, we find that political consciousness among the *Dalits* "which allow pride, self-respect and a vision of the future"[20] is not only getting politically articulated but its multifarious manifestations including the literary one are political in nature and formed through process of political socialisation, mobilisation and participation actively in the *Dalit* movement, undermining decisively the traditional caste hierarchy of a social order that has made them subjugated for centuries. The *Dalit* Literary expression hence becomes political that challenges supremacy of the upper castes in all walks of life and thereby making efforts "for better access to the opportunities, and for gaining self-respect and dignified social identities."[21]

NOTES

1. Gajendran, A. *'Transforming Dalit Politics'* in Seminar (November, 1998 issue) Delhi p. 24.
2. Zelliot, Elanor. *'The Roots of Dalit Consciousness'* in Seminar, *Ibid*, p. 28-29.
3. Shah, Ghanshyam. *'Dalit Movments and the Search for Identity'* in Ghanshyam Shah (ed.) '*Dalit* Identity and Politics (Delhi: Sage Publications, 2001) p. 195.
4. Please see Introduction and other articles of the Special Issue of *Seminar* (December 2001) on Caste, Race and *Dalit* Question for further detail.
5. *Ibid.*
6. *Ibid.* p. 31-32.
7. Please see the Bhopal Document and Declaration 2002 published by the Government of Madhya Pradesh for further detail.
8. *Ibid.*
9. *Ibid.*
10. *Ibid.*
11. Bharati, Kanwal. *Dalit Vimarsh Ki Bhumika* (Allahabad: Itihas Bodh Prakashan, 2001) p. 109.
12. *Ibid.*
13. *Ibid.* p. 135.
14. Limbale, Sharan Kumar. *Ibid.* p. 29.
15. *Ibid.* p. 112.
16. Pantawane, Gangadhar. In *Asmitadars* quoted in Eleanor Zelliot, *Ibid.* p. 268.
17. Please see Joseph Benjamin, *Ibid.* for further detail.
18. Guru, Gopal. *Ibid.* p. 31-2.
19. Please see Bhopal Document and Declaration for further detail.
20. Zelliot. Eleanor. *'The Roots of Dalit Consciousness' Ibid.* p. 28-29.
21. Ram, Nandu. *Ibid.*

ANNEXURE

Constitutional and Legal Safeguards

Article 15 prohibits discrimination on grounds of religion, race, caste, sex or place of birth. Clause 1 states; "The State shall not discriminate against any citizen on grounds only of religion, race, caste, sex, place of birth or any of them. Clause 2 states "No citizen shall, on grounds only of religion, race, caste, sex, place of birth or any of them be subjected to any disability, liability, restriction or condition with regard to:

(*a*) Access to shops, public restaurants, hotels and place of public entertainments; or
(*b*) The use of wells, tanks, bathing *ghats*, roads and places of public resort maintained wholly or partly out of State funds or dedicated to the use of the general public

Clause 3 states nothing in this Article or in Clause 2 of Article 29 shall prevent the State from making any special provision for the advancement of any socially and educationally backward classes of citizens or for the Scheduled Castes and the Scheduled Tribes vide 1st Amendment Act, 1951.

Article 16, Clause 4 highlights, "Nothing in this article shall prevent the State from making any provision for the reservation of appointments or posts in favour of any backward class of citizens which, in the opinion of the State, is not adequately represented in the services under the State.

Article 17 states, "Untouchability is abolished and its practice in any form is forbidden. The enforcement of any disability arising out of 'untochability' shall be an offence punishable in accordance with law.

Article 19, Clause 1, sub-clause (g) provides the right to practise any profession, or to carry on any occupation trade or business.

Article 23, Clause 1, states, "Traffic in human beings and *begar* and other similar forms of forced labour are prohibited and any contravention of this provision shall be an offence punishable in accordance with law.

Article 25, Clause 2, sub-clause (*b*) states, "Nothing in this article shall affect the operation of any existing law or prevent the State from making any law providing for social welfare and reform or the throwing open of Hindu religious institutions of a public character to all classes and sections of Hindus".

Article 29, Clause 2 refers "No citizen shall be denied admission into any educational institution maintained by the State or receiving aid out of State funds on grounds only of religion., race caste, language or any of them."

Article 38, Clause 2 states "The State shall, in particular, strive to minimise the inequalities in income and endeavour to eliminate inequalities in status, facilities and opportunities, not only among individuals, but also amongst groups of people residing in different areas or engaged in different vocations".

Article 46 states, "The State shall promote with special care the educational and economic interests of the weaker sections of the people, and, in particular, of the Scheduled Castes and the Scheduled Tribes, and shall protect them from social injustice and all forms of exploitation".

Article 164, Clause 1, keeps the provision that in the State of Bihar, Madhya Pradesh and Orissa, there shall be a minister in charge of tribal welfare who may in addition be in charge of the welfare of the Schedule Castes and backward classes or any other work.

Article 330, Clauses 2 states, "The number of seats reserved in any State or Union Territory for the Scheduled Castes or Scheduled Tribes under clause 1 shall bear, as nearly as may be, the same proportion to the total number of seats allotted to that State or Union Territory in the house of the people as the population of the Scheduled Castes in the States or the Union Territory or of the Scheduled Tribes in the State or Union Territory or part of the State or Union Territory as the case may be, in respect of which seats are so reserved, bears to the total population of the State".

There are temporary provisions for special representation of and reservations of seats for Scheduled Castes and Scheduled Tribes in the Legislatures (Articles 330, 332, 334).

Article 335 states that claim of Scheduled Castes and Scheduled

Tribes shall be taken into consideration, consistently with the maintenance of efficiency of administration, in the making of appointments to services and posts in connection with the affairs of the Union or of a State.

Article 338 Clause 1 states, "There shall be special officer for the Scheduled Castes and Scheduled Tribes to be appointed by the President Clauses 2. It shall be the duty of the special officer to investigate all matters relating to the safeguards provided for the Scheduled Castes and Scheduled Tribes under this Constitution and report to the President upon the working of those safeguards at such intervals as the President may direct, and the President shall cause all such reports to be laid before each House of Parliament. As to Clause 3 in this Article reference to the Scheduled Castes and Scheduled Tribes shall be construed as including reference to such other backward classes as the President may, on receipt of the report of a Commission appointed under Clauses 1 of Article 340, by order specify and also to the Anglo-Indian Community.

According to Article 341 Clause 1 The President may with respect to any State (or Union Territory) and where it is a State after Consultation with the Governor.thereof, by public notification, specify the castes, races or tribes or parts of or groups within castes, races or tribes which shall for the purpose of this Constitution be deemed to be Scheduled Castes in relation to that State (or Union Territory, as the case may be). Clause 2 says Parliament by law may include in or exclude from the list of Scheduled Castes specified in a notification issued under clause 1 any caste, race or tribe or part of or group within any caste, race or tribe, but save as aforesaid a notification issued under the said clause shall not be varied by any subsequent notifications.

Article 366 states, in the Constitution, unless the context otherwise requires, the following expressions have the meanings hereby respectively assigned to them, that is to say: according to clause 24 'Scheduled Castes' means such castes and races or tribes as are deemed under Article 341 to be Scheduled Castes for the purpose of this Constitution.

Bibliography

Primary Texts

Balmiki, Om Prakash. *Joothan* (Delhi: Radha Krishan Prakashan, 1997).

Bhandari, Mannu. *Maha Bhoj* (Delhi: Radha Krishna Prakashan, 1979, twenty fourth edition, 1999) and English translation *The Great Feast* by Richard Allan Williams (Delhi: Radha Krishna Prakashan, 1981).

Chandra, Jagdish. *Dharati Dhan Na Apana* (Delhi: Rajkamal Prakashan, 1972, Paperback 1996).

Chauhan, Suraj Pal. *Harry Kab Aayega* (Sahibabad: Anubhav Prakashan, 1999).

Kardam, Jai Prakash. *Gunga Nahin Tha Main* (Delhi: Aatish Prakashan, 1997).

Nagar, Amrit Lal. *Nachyo Bahut Gopal* (Delhi: Rajpal & Sons, 1999 edition).

Naimishray, Mohan Dass. *Apne Apne Pinjare* (Delhi: Vani Prakashan, 1995).

Premchand. *Godan* (Delhi: Rajkamal Paperbacks, 1988) and English translation by Jai Ratan and P. Lal (Bombay: Jaico Publishing House, 1991, eleventh impression).

Premchand. *Kafan* from edited collection by Bhisma Sahni. *Premchand: Pratinidhi Kahaniyan* (Delhi: Rajkamal Paperbacks 1987).

'Rahi', Lalchand. *Kranti Shesh Hai* (Ujjain: Madhya Pradesh Dalit Sahitya Academy, 1995).

Singh, Malkhan. *Suno Brahaman* (Rampur: Bodhisattva Prakashan, 1996).

Abrams. M.H. *A Glossary of Literary Terms* (Delhi: Macmillan, 1978).

Adorno, T.W. *Aesthetic Theory* (Trns: C. Ienhardt, eds: Gretel Adorno & Rolf Tidemann) (London: Routledge & Kegan Paul, 1984).

Ahir, D.C. *Life of Dr.Ambedkar* (Delhi: B.R. Publishing Corporation, 1990).

Ahmed, Aijaz. *In Theory: Classes, Narrations, Literatures* (Delhi: Oxford University Press, 1994).

Ambedkar, B.R. (1979), *Castes in India: their Mechanism and Development (1917); Annihilation of Caste (1936)* reprinted in *Dr.Babasaheb Ambedkar: Writings and Speeches*, Vol. I. Government of Maharashtra, Bombay.

Ambedkar, B.R. (1990) *Mr. Gandhi and the Emancipation of the Untouchables (1943); What Congress and Gandhi have done to the Untouchables (1945)* in *Dr.Babasaheb Ambedkar: Writings and Speeches*, Vol.9. Government of Maharashtra, Bombay.

Ambedkar, B.R. (1990) *Who were Shudras? (1946) and The Untouchables (1948)* in *Dr.Babasaheb Ambedkar: Writings and Speeches*, Vol. 7. Government of Maharashtra, Bombay.

Anand, M.R. *Untouchable* (Delhi: Mayfair Paperbacks, 1981).
Andrew, Joe. *Writers and Society During the Rise of Russian Revolution* (London: MacMillan, 1980).
Baxi, U. and Parikh, B. (eds.) *Crisis and Change in Contemporary India* (Delhi: Sage Publications, 1995).
'Bechain', Sheoraj Singh and Choubey, Devendra (eds.). *Chintan Ki Parampara Aur Dalit Sahitya* (Hazaribagh: Navlakhan Prakashan, 2000-1).
Benjamin, J. *Scheduled Caste in Indian Politics and Society* (Delhi: Ess Ess Publications, 1989).
Beteille, A. *Caste, Class and Power* (Delhi: Oxford University Press, 1966).
Beteille, A. *Inequality and Social Change* (Delhi: Oxford University Press, 1972).
Bharati, Kanwal. *Dalit Vimarsh Ki Bhumika* (Allahabad: Itihas Bodh Prakashan, year not mentioned).
Boggs, Carl. *Gramsci's Marxis.*(London: Pluto Press, 1976).
Bosanquet, Bernard. *History of Aesthetics* (London: Allan & Unwin, 1966).
Brass, P.R. *Caste, Faction and Party in Indian Politics 2 vlms.* (Delhi: Chanakya Publications, 1985).
Brass, P.R. *The Politics of India since Independence* (Cambridge: Cambridge University Press, 1990).
Burman, B.K. Roy. *Beyond Mandal and After: Backward Classes in Perspective* (Delhi: Mittal Publications, 1992).
Caudwell, Christopher. *Illusion and Reality: A Study of the Sources of Poetry* (Delhi: People's Publication House, 1945, reprinted in 1991).
Chatterjee, P. *The Nation and Its Fragments: Colonial and Post-Colonial Histories* (Delhi: Oxford University Press, 1993).
Chauhan, B.R. *Scheduled Castes and Education* (Meerut: Anu Publications, 1975).
Choubey, Devendra. *Kathakar Amrit Lal Nagar* (Delhi: Jagat Ram & Sons, 1994).
Collingwood, R.G. *The Principles of Art* (Oxford: Oxford University Press, 1947).
Dahl, Robert. *Modern Political Analysis* (Delhi: Prentice Hall of Indian, 1991, fifth edition).
Dahrendorf, R. *Class and Class Conflict in Industrial Society* (Stanford: Stanford University Press, 1957).
Desai, A.R. *Social Background of Indian Nationalism* (Bombay: Popular Prakashan, 1959).
Dharmveer. *Kabir Ke Aalochak* (Delhi: Vani Prakashan, 1998, second edition).
Dube, S.C. *Contemporary India and Its Modernisation* (Delhi: Vikas Publishing House, 1974).
Dube, S.C. *Indian Society* (Delhi: National Book Trust, 1990).
Dumont, L. *Homo Hierarchicus: The Caste System and Its Implications* (London: Paladin, 1970).
Eagleton, Terry. *Marxism and Other Essays* (London: Methuen & Co., 1976, Reprinted, 1983) .

Eagleton, Terry. *Criticism and Ideology: A Study in Marxist Literary Theory* (London: Verso, 1986).

Eagleton, Terry. The Ideology of the Aesthetics (Oxford: Basil Blackwell, 1991).

Fernades, W. *The Emerging Dalit Identities* (Delhi: Indian Social Institute, 1996).

Frankel, F. and M.S.A.RAO *Dominance and State Power in Modern India: A Decline of Social Order* (Delhi: Oxford University Press, 1989) .

Fuchs, S. *At the Botton of Indian Society: Harijans and Other Lower Castes* (Delhi: Munshiram Manoharlal Publishers, 1981).

Galanter, M. *Competing Equalities: Law and the Backward Classes in India* (Berkeley: University of California Press, 1984).

Georg, Lukacs. *History and Class Consciousness* (Delhi: Rupa & Co., 1993).

Ghurye, G.S. *Caste and Class in India* (Bombay: Popular Book Depot, 1957).

Goldmann, Lucien. *Method in the Sociology of Literature* (Translated William Q. Boelhower) (Oxford: Basil Blackwell Publisher, 1980) .

Gore, M.S. *Social Context of an Ideology: Ambedkar's Social and Political Thought* (Delhi: Sage Publications, 1993).

Gramsci, Antonio. *The Prison Notebooks* (London: Lawrence & Wishart, 1971).

Green, Philip and Walzer Michael (eds). *The Political Imagination in Literature: A Reader* (New York: The Free Press, 1969).

Gupta, P.C. *Literature and Society: Selected Essays* (Delhi: People's Publishing House, 1983).

Gupta, Prakash Chandra. *Premchand* (Delhi: Sahitya Academy, 1968).

Gupta, Ramanika. *Dalit Chetna: Sooch* (Hazaribagh: Navlakhen Prakashan, 1998).

Gupta, S.K. *Scheduled Castes in Modern Indian Politics: Their Emergence as a Political Power* (Delhi: Munshiram Manoharlal Publishers, 1985).

Harap, Louis. *Social Roots of the Arts* (New York: International Publishers, 1949).

Hasan, Z. *Dominance and Mobilisation: Rural Politics in Western Uttar Pradesh*, (Delhi: Sage Publications, 1989).

Hasan, Z. *Gandhi and the Harijans* (Delhi: Shree Publishing House, 1986).

Ilaiah, Kancha. *Why I am not a Hindu: Am Sudra Critique of Hindutva Philosophy, Culture and Political Economy* (Calcutta: SAMYA, 1996).

Jameson, Fredrick. *Marxism and Form—Twentieth Century Dialectical Theories of Literature* (Princeton: Princeton University Press, 1978).

Jhanji, Rekha. Communication and the Arts (Delhi: Ajanta Publishers, 1984).

Jogdand, P.G. *Dalit Movement in Maharashtra* (Delhi: Kanak Publications, 1991).

Johri, J.C. *Comparative Politics* (Delhi: Sterling Publishers, 1972).

Joshi, B. *Democracy in Search of Equality: Untouchable Politics and Indian Social Change* (Delhi: Hindustan Publications, 1982).

Joshi, B.R.(ed.). *Untouchable! Voices of the Dalit Liberation Movement* (London: Zed and MRG, 1986).

Juergensmeyer, M. *Religion as Social Vision: the Movement against Untouchability in 20th Century Punjab* (Berkley, University of California Press, 1982).

Kamble, J.R. *Rise and Awakening of Depressed Classes in India* (Delhi: National Publishing House, 1979).

Keer, D. *Dr. Ambedkar: Life and Mission* (Bombay: Popular Prakashan, 1962).
Khare, R.S. *The Untouchable as Himself: Ideology and Pragmatism among Lucknow Chamars* (London: Cambridge Press, 1984).
Klarer, Mario. *An Introduction to Literary Studies* (London: Routledge, 1999).
Kothari, R. *Caste in Indian Politics* (Hyderabad: Orient-Longman, 1970).
Kothari, R. *Politics in India* (Delhi: Orient-Longman, 1970).
Kshirsagar, R.K. *Dalit Movement and Its Leaders 1857-1956* (Delhi: M.D. Publishers, 1994).
Limbale. Sharan Kumar. *Dalit Sahitya Ka Saundaryashastra* (translated by Ramanika Gupta) (Delhi: Vani Prakashan, 2000).
Lipson, Leslie. *The Great Issues of Politics: An Introduction to Political Science* (Delhi: Prentice-Hall of India, 1993, Ninth edition).
Louis, Prakash. *Casteism is Horrendous then Racism: Durban and Dalit Discourse* (Delhi: Indian Social Institute, 2001).
Lowenthal, Leo. *Literature and the Image of Man* (London: Methuen & Co., 1975).
Lukacs, Georg. *Studies in European Realism* (New York: Grosset & Dunlop, 1964).
Lynch, Owen M. *The Politics of Untouchability: Social Mobility and Social Change in a City of India* (New York: Columbia University Press, 1969).
Markandeya and Mishra, Satyaprakash (eds). *Premchand Ki Kahaniyon Ka Mahatav* (Allahabad: Sumit Prakashan, 1998).
Marx K. & Engels, F. *Communist Manifesto* (Moscow: Progress Publishers, 1977).
Marx, K., Engels, F. *On Literature and Art* (Moscow: Progress Publishers, 1976).
Mendelsohn, O. and Baxi, U. (eds.) *The Rights of Subordinated Peoples* (Delhi: Oxford University Press, 1994).
Mishra, Vidhya Niwas. *Sahitya Ka Saundaryashastra* (Chandigarh: Haryana Sahitya Academy, 1997).
Mukherjee, Meenakshi. *Realism and Reality: The Novel and Society in India* (Delhi: Oxford University Press, 1985).
Mukherjee, Sujit. *Towards a Literary History of India* (Simla: Indian Institute of Advanced Studies, 1975).
Nagendra (ed). *Premchand: An Antholgy* (Delhi: Bansal & Co. 1981).
Omvedt, G. *Dalit Vision* (Delhi: Orient-Longman, 1995).
Omvedt, Gail. *Dalits and the Democratic Revolution: Dr. Ambedkar and the Dalit Movement in Colonial India* (Delhi: Sage Publications, 1994).
Oommen, T.K. *Protest and Social Change: Studies in Social Movements* (Delhi: Sage Publications, 1990).
Pai, Sudha. *State Politics: New Dimensions* (Delhi: Shipra Publications, 2000).
Pai.Sudha *UP: Agrarian Change and Electoral Politics* (Delhi: Shipra Publications, 1993).
Pandey, Manager. *Sahitya Ke Samajshastra Ki Bhoomika* (Chandigarh: Haryana

Sahitya Academy, 1989).

Phule, Jotirao. (Translated by, Daya Agarwal) (Delhi: National Book Trust, 1996).

Phule, Jotirao. *Gulaamgiri* (translated by Vimal Kirti, ed. by Jai Prakash Kardam) (Delhi: Sangeeta Prakashan, 1995).

Pinto, A. Dalit Christians: A Socio-economic Survey. Bangalore: Aashirvad, Centre for Non-Formal and Continuing Education, 1992.

Pinto, Ambrose. *Dalits: Assertion for Identity* (Delhi: Indian Social Institute, 1999).

Quigley, D. *The Interpretation of Caste* (Delhi: Oxford University Press, 1993).

Rai, Amrit. *Premchand: His Life and Times* (Translated. Harish Trivedi) (Delhi: Oxford University Press, 1982).

Rajkishore (ed.) *Harijan Se Dalit* (Delhi: Vani Prakashan, 1995, second edition).

Rajkishore. *Jati Kaun Todega* (Delhi: Praksahan Sansthan, 2000, second edition).

Ram, Nandu. *Beyond Ambedkar: Essays on Dalits in India* (Delhi: Har-Anand Publications, 1995).

Ram, Nandu. *The Mobile Scheduled Castes: Rise of a New Middle Class* (Delhi: Hindustan Publishing Corporation, 1988).

Rao, M.S.A. *Social Movements in India* 2 vlms. (Delhi: Manohar Publications, 1978-79).

Robb, P. *Dalit Movement and the Meanings of Labour in India* (Delhi: Oxford University Press, 1993).

Robson, W.W. *The Definition of Literature and Other Essays* (Cambridge: Cambridge University Press, 1982).

Rudolph, L.T. and S.H. Rudolph *In Pursuit of Laxmi* (Delhi: Orient-Longman, 1987).

Rudolph, L.T. and S.H. Rudolph *The Modernity of Tradition: The Political Developments in India* (Chicago: University of Chicago Press, 1967).

Sabine, George H. *A History of Political Theory* (Calcutta: Oxford and IBH Publishing Co., 1937, Third edition, 1961).

Satyamurthy, T.V. (ed.) *Region, Religion, Caste, Gender and Culture in Contemporary India* (Delhi: Oxford University Press, 1996).

Satyendra (ed). *Premchand* (Delhi: Radha Krishna, 1976, Fourth edition, 1998).

Shah, G. *Protest Movements in Two Indian States* (Delhi: Ajanta Publications, 1977).

Shah, G. *Social Movements in India: A Review of Literature* (Delhi: Sage Publications, 1990).

Shah, Ghanshyam (ed). *Dalit Identity and Politics* (Delhi: Sage Publications, 2001).

Shahi, Sadanand (ed). *Dalit Sahitya Ke Avdharana Aur Premchand* (Gorakahpur: Premchand Sahitya Sansthan, 2000).

Shahi, Sadanand (ed). *Premchand Ki Kahaniyan: Sadagi Ka Saundaryasashtra* (Allahabad: Abhivyaki Prakashan, 2000).

Shahi, Sadanand. *Godan Me Dalit Prasang Ke Nihitarth* (Gorakahpur: Premchand Sahitya Sansthan, year not mentioned).

Sharma, K.L. (ed.) *Caste and Class in India* (Jaipur: Rawat Publications, 1994).

Shrivastava, Parmanand. *Godan: Ek Punarvichar* (Allahabad: Abhivyaki Prakashan, 1999).

Sibley, Mulford Q. *Political Ideas and Ideologies* (Delhi: Surjeet Publications, 1981).

Singh, Bacchan. *Sahitya Ka Samajshastra* (Allahabad: Lok Bharati Prakasha, 1998, second edition) .

Singh, Y. *Modernisations of Indian Tradition* (Delhi: Thomson Press, 1973).

Srinivas, M.N. (ed.) *Caste: Its Twentieth Century Avatar* (Delhi: Viking, 1996).

Srinivas, M.N. *Caste in Modern India and Other Essays* (Bombay: Media Frontiers, 1962).

Srinivas, M.N. *Cohesive Role of Sanskritization and Other Essays* (Delhi: Oxford University Press, 1986).

Srinivas, M.N. *Social Change in Modern India* (Bombay: Allied Publishers, 1966).

Trilling, L. *The Liberal Imagination—Essays on Literature and Society* (London: Secker and Warburg, 1951).

Varma, S.P. *Modern Political Analysis* (Delhi: Vikas Publishing House, 1975).

Williams, Raymond. *Keywords: A Vocabulary of Culture and Society* (London: Fontana Press, 1976).

Williams, Raymond. *Marxism and Literature* (Oxford: Oxford University Press, 1977).

Zelliot, E. *From Untouchable to Dalit: Essays on Ambedkar Movement* (Delhi: Manohar Publications, 1992).

Zwick, E. *Literature and Liberalism* (Washington, D.C.: The New Republic Book Co., 1970).

Articles

Berreman, G. The Brahmanical View of Caste. *Contributions to Indian Sociology* (N.S.) 5 1971: 16-23.

Chatterjee, M. Divided They Fall: SP-BSP Split Helps the BJP in UP. *Frontline*, June 28, 1996.

Dolgov, K.M. Aesthetics of Georg Lukacs. *The Polish Philosophical Quarterly.* Vol. xv, no. 8, 1-2, 1988.

Gaikwad, S.M. Ambedkar and Indian Nationalism. *Economic and Political Weekly* 33(10): 7 March 1998.

Gehlot, N.S. Dr. Ambedkar, Mahatama Gandhi and Dalit movement. *Indian Journal of Political Science* 54(3-4): July-December 1993.

Gupta, Dipankar. Positive Discrimination and the Question of Fraternity: Contrasting Ambedkar and Mandal on Reservations. *Economic and Political Weekly* 32(31): 2 August 1997.

Guru, G. Dalit Movement in Mainstream Sociology. *Economic and Political Weekly*, April 3, 1993.

Guru, G. Dalit Resurrection. *Hindu*, Feb. 16, 1996.

Guru, G. Understanding Violence, against Dalits in Marathwada. *Economic and Political Weekly*, Feb. 26, 1994.

Kothari, R. Rise of Dalits and the Renewed Debate on Caste. *Economic and Political Weekly*, June 25, 1994.

Kothari, Rajni. Rise of the Dalits and the Renewed Debate on Caste. *Economic and Political Weekly* 29(26): 25 June 1994.

Mendelsohn, O. The Transformation of Authority in Rural India. *Modern Asian Studies* 27: 1993:805-42.

Nadkarni, M.V. Broad basing Process in India and Dalits: *Economic and Political Weekly* 32(33-34): 1997:2260-71.

Omvedt, G. *Ambedkarism: The Theory of Dalit Liberation. Frontiers*, 25(12 & 13); 21 October 1992.

Omvedt, G. Peasants, Dalits and Women: Democracy and India's New Social Movement', *Journal of Contemporary Asia*, 24(1): 1994.

Padgaonkar, D. Ambedkar and Gandhi: the Antagonism of Profound Significance. *Times of India* (Delhi Ed.) April 14, 1990.

Pai, S. and J. Singh Politicisation of Dalits and Most Backward Castes. *Economic and Political Weekly*, June 7, 1997.

Pai, Sudha and Jagpal Singh. Politicisation of Dalits and Most Backward Castes: Study of Social Conflict and Political Preferences in Four Villages of Meerut district. *Economics and Political Weekly* 32(23): 7 June 1997.

Pandit, Nalin. Ambedkar and the Dalits. *Seminar* (461), Annual: January 1998.

Patnaik, Arun Kumar. Dalit Common Sense against Hindutva. *Economic and Political Weekly* 31(40): 2 November 1996.

Prashad, V. The Untouchable Question. *Economic and Political Weekly* 32(9): 1996:551-59.

Pratap, Vijay. Dalit Consciousness, Voluntary Work and Social Change. *Janata* 50(1-4) Annual No.: 1995.

Punalekar S.P. Dalitism and Gender. *Third Concept* 8(90): August 1994.

Ramaseshan, R. Dalit Politics in U.P. *Seminar*, January, 1995.

Satyanarayana. A. Dalit Protest Literature in Telugu: A Historical Perspective. *Economic and Political Weekly* 30(3): 21 January 1995:171-75.

Webester, C.B. (1995) Towards Understanding the Modern Dalit Movement. First Ambedkar Chair Lecture, School of Social Sciences, Jawaharlal Nehru University, New Delhi.

Zelliot, E. Dalit Culture and Social Action *Frontiers*, 25(15): March 21, 1992.

Census/Declarations

Census of India (1981-91) *Primary Census Abstracts Scheduled Castes and Tribes: Social and Cultural Tables*, and also *Special Tables for the Scheduled Castes and Tribes*, Government of India, Delhi.

Census of India (1993) *Union Primary Census Abstract for Scheduled Castes and Scheduled Tribes*, Paper I, Government of India, Delhi.

Census of India (1993) *Literacy Trends in the 1980's in India*-Occasional Papers No. 4 for Census of India, 1991, Government of India, Delhi.

The Bhopal Document (2002) Government of Madhya Pradesh, Bhopal.
The Bhopal Declaration (2002) Government of Madhya Pradesh, Bhopal .
The Durban Declaration (2001) United Nations.

Journals/Magazines/Newspapers

Aaj Kal (Hindi), Delhi.
Aalochana (Hindi), Delhi.
Amar Ujala (Hindi), Meerut.
Ambedkar in India (Hindi), Kushinagar.
Bahuvachan (Hindi), Delhi.
Dalit Jan Ubhaar (Hindi), Lucknow.
Dalit Sahitya, 1999 to 2002 (Hindi), Delhi.
Dalit Voice, Delhi.
Danik Jagran (Hindi), Allahabad.
Economic and Political Weekly, Bombay.
Frontline, Chennai.
Hans (Hindi), Delhi.
Hindustan Times, Delhi.
India Today, Delhi.
Kathakram (Hindi), Lucknow.
Mainstream, Delhi.
Nukkad: Janam Samvad (Hindi), Delhi.
Outlook, Delhi.
Rashtriya Sahara (Hindi), Lucknow.
Samaya Drishti (Hindi), Delhi.
Sanchetna (Hindi), Delhi.
Seminar, Delhi.
The Hindu, Chennai.
Times of India, Delhi.
Vartman Sahitya (Hindi), Ghaziabad.
Yudhrat Aam Aadami (Hindi), Hazaribagh.

Unpublished Thesis/Dissertations

Harijan, Raj Kumar. (1993) *Forms of Oppression: Caste, Class and Ethnicity: Am Study of Three Text* (Untouchable (M.R. Anand); *Godan* (Premchand); Paraja (Gopinath Mohanty). Centre of Linguistics and English, School of Languages, Literature and Culture Studies, Jawaharlal Nehru University, Delhi.

Jogdand, P.G. (1981) *From Discrimination to Movement: A Study of Dalit Movement in Maharashtra*, Centre for the Study of Social Systems, School of Social Sciences, Jawaharlal Nehru University, Delhi.

Kumar, Abhay. (1998). *Dalit Atmakatha Ki Parampara Aur Apne Apne Pinjare*

Centre of Indian Languages, School of Languages, Literature and Culture Studies, Jawaharlal Nehru University, Delhi.

Manjulata. (1986). *Mahabhoj Me Samajik Chetna* Centre of Indian Languages, School of Languages, Literature and Culture Studies, Jawaharlal Nehru University, Delhi.

Paswan, Rajesh Kumar (1999). *Dalit Atmaabhivakti Aur Joothan*. Centre of Indian Languages, School of Languages, Literature and Culture Studies, Jawaharlal Nehru University, Delhi.

Prasad, Dayanada. (1999) *Jagdish Chandra Ke Katha Sahitya Me Dalit Chetna,* Centre of Indian Languages, School of Languages, Literature and Culture Studies, Jawaharlal Nehru University, Delhi.

Pullarao, Y. (1990) *Dalit Ideology: An Examination of Some Issues*, Centre for Political Studies, School of Social Sciences, Jawaharlal Nehru University, Delhi.

Index

21 Point Action Agenda 149
Abdullah, Sheikh 123
Acchutanand, Swami 19, 45, 46, 79, 84, 91, 101, 155
Adi Hindu 45–46
    Ideology 84
    Movement 45
Adi-Dharma movement 65–66
Ahmed, Manjoor 127
All-India Depressed Classes Conference 70, 73, 83
All-India Scheduled Castes Federation 102
Alternative Movement 61
Althusser, Louis 37
Ambedkar, B.R. 3, 6, 19, 45, 46, 47, 56, 61, 67, 69, 70, 71, 73, 74, 77, 84, 85, 86, 87, 100, 101, 102, 106, 110, 112, 122, 123, 127, 130, 136, 141, 145, 147, 149, 155, 159
    Movement 48, 77
    Scheduled Castes Federation 66
Ambesh, Chatrapati 47
Andhra Pradesh 68
Anglo-Indian Community 164
Anti-caste
    Ideology 103
    Literature 45
Anti-colonial Struggle 6, 144
Anti-Dalit Story 92
Anti-Untouchability Movements 66
Aristotle 24, 30
Arya Samaj 46, 65, 101
Arya Samaj Shuddhi Campaign 84
Association for the Maintenance of Dharma 67
Backward and Minorities Communities Employees Federation 121
Bacon, Francis 25
Bagadi, Mani Ram 127
Bahujan Samaj Party 121, 145–46
Balmiki, Om Prakash 8, 10, 45, 91, 133, 134, 136, 140, 154
Banodha, Ramchand 47
Begar 95, 162
Besant, Annie 52
Bhakti 44, 64
    Movement 19, 43–45, 61–65, 67, 79
    Period 75
    Resurgence 84
    Songs 62
    Tradition 63, 65
Bhandari, Mannu 8, 10, 114
Bharati, Kanwal 79, 91, 100, 154
Bharti, Maharaj Singh 127
Bhisma Sahni 90
Bhopal Declaration 153–54, 160
Bihar 68
Biographical Literary Criticism 29
Boelhower, William Q. 32
Bohre, Khemchand 47
Bonded Labour System (Abolition) Act 151
Brahmanism 99–100, 136, 147, 158
    Caste System 85
    Ideology 59
    Social Norms 85
British Colonialism 93
Buddha 130, 155, 159
Buddhism 67, 79, 102

Capitalism 93–94
Caste
Based Discriminations 160
Literature 80
Oppression 2
Ridden Society 47
System 1, 65, 75–76, 78, 85–87, 159
Caudwell, Christopher 37
Census Report 52
Chandra, Jagdish 8, 10, 101, 103, 104
Chandra, Sarat 135
Charan, Baba Ram 46, 84, 101
Chauhan, Suraj Pal 8, 10, 140, 141, 154, 160
Chokhamela 3, 19, 62, 76
Chowdhry, Surendra 90
Christian
Literature 79
Movement 146
Civil Disobedience 83
Civil Society, Ideals of 149
Colonialism 85
Communal Award 72, 83
Congress 70, 121
Constitution of India 54, 71, 149, 151
Contemporary Literature 21
Conversion Movement 67–69
Counter-Cultural Movements 60
Critical Theory 34
Croce, Beneditto 23, 26

Dahl, Robert 16
Dalit
Activism 137
Aesthetics 7, 80
Assertion 157
Community 17–18, 42, 52, 158
Cultural Movement 45
Empowerment 136, 159
Issue 45
Liberation 55, 67, 91, 101
Literature 4–8, 10, 18, 22, 39–40, 42–45, 47–49, 68, 79–80, 91–92, 102, 141, 146, 148, 154–55, 160
Movement 3–7, 9, 40–48, 53, 56–57, 60–61, 65, 67, 69–70, 74–78, 83–87, 90–91, 102, 131, 137–38, 144–48, 156–61
Panthers 2–3, 20, 53, 137
Politics 45, 47
Struggle 77
Upliftment 113
Writers 6
Dalits Shoshit Samaj Sangharsh Samiti 121
Defamiliarization 30
Depressed Classes 52–54, 70
Dhasal, Namdev 68
Dialectical Materialism 34
Diksha 67
Durban Conferences 160
Dyaneshwar 44

Eagleton, Terry 37
Ecological Model of Research 9
Egalitarian Society 21, 45
Empiricism 4, 25, 27–28
Employment of Manual Scavengers and Construction 152
English Literature 21
Equality and Solidarity 21

Feudalism 93–94
Fischer, Ernst 37
Formalism 4–5, 29–30
Branches of 30
Formalist 6, 23
School 31
Form-based Studies 8
Frankfurt School 34, 40
Frazer, J.G 31
Free and High Quality Education 151
Freedom Struggle 69, 85, 87, 94
Frye, Northrop 31

Gandhi, Mahatma 6, 44, 45, 52
Gandhi-Irwin Pact 83
Gandhiji vs. Dr. Ambedkar 72
Gherao 58
Ghurye, G.S. 1
Global Literature 79
Godan 86, 92
Golden Bough 31
Goldmann, Lucien 31, 32, 33, 41
Government of India Act 52, 54, 72, 83
Gupta, Jagdish 79
Guru Nanak 47
Guru, Gopal 45, 148
Guru, Sri Narayana 155

Harijan 2, 52
Harijan Sevak Sangh 72
Hartal 58
Hegel, G.W.F. 25
Hindi Dalit Literature 6
Hindu
- Caste System 136, 141, 160
- Intellectual Tradition 68
- Mahasabha 69

Hinduism 76, 147
Holistic Representation 94
Human Activities, Concepts of 17
Human Existence, Feature of 14
Hutton, J.H. 54

Idealism 23, 86, 158
Identity-Building Process 61
Imperialism 85
Independent Labour Party 20, 73
Indian Caste System 7, 43
- Features of 1

Indian National Congress 72, 102, 108, 122
Intuition-expression 27

Jatava Youth League 102
Juergensmeyer, Mark 66
Justice Party 67

Kabir 3, 19, 47, 76, 85, 130, 159
Kain, Babu Karan Singh 47
Kant, Immanuel 25
Kardam, Jai Prakash 8, 10, 79, 141
Karnataka 68
Keer, Dhananjay 47
Kerala 68
Knowledge Transmission 56
Kothari, Rajni 59, 77

Lalchand 'Rahi' 8, 10, 129
Lawani (Ballads) 43
League against Untouchability 72
Liberty, Principles of 21
Limbale, Sharan Kumar 47, 80, 155
Literary
- Criticism 5, 30, 33–34, 41
- Revival 64
- Theory 41

Literature, Critics of 29
Lukacs 32, 38
Lukacs, Georg 38

Macro-Analytical Categories 32
Madhya Pradesh Dalit Sahitya Academy 129
Mahar
- Conference 67
- Movement 43

Maharaj, Eknath 3, 19, 62, 63, 76
Maharashtrian anti-caste Stayashodhak Samaj 1
Marathi
- Dalit Literature 44–45, 85, 137
- Literature 44
- Writing 44

Marathwada University 137
Marx, Karl 36
Marxism 39
Marxist 5–6
- Criticism 35–36
- Ideology 59, 136
- Literary Criticism 37, 39–40, 158
- Literary Theory 35
- School 35

Maurya, B.P. 123, 127
Mayawati 146
Meghdoot Natya Samstha 137
Mehta, Narasimha 52
Meta Narrative Consciousness 23
Minimum Wages Act 74
Moneylenders 95
Movements for Better Access 48
Mukherjee, Meenakshi 89, 96
Muslim League 69
Myth Criticism 31

Nagar, Amrit Lal 8, 10, 79, 108, 109, 124
Naikar, E.V. Periyar Swami 155
Naimishray, Mohan Dass 8, 10, 45, 47, 122, 123, 124, 125, 126, 127, 128, 140, 141, 154
Namashudra Movements 66
National and State Commissions for SCs and STs 151
National Freedom 93
National Liberation Movement 42, 83, 85, 108, 130
Nationalist Literature 79
Nehru, Jawaharlal 123
Neo-Vedantic Movement 62, 65, 67
New Criticism 30
Non-Brahman movement 65, 75
Non-Cooperation movement 85

Pai, Sudha 102, 134
Pantavane, Gangadhar 53, 68
Pawads (Panegyric poetry) 43
Phule, Mahatma Jotiba 19, 47, 130, 155, 159
Piaget, J. 32
Pippal, Gopi Chand 47
Plato 23, 24
Political
    Consciousness 3, 8, 13–14, 19, 48
    Development of the Community 19
    Literature 5
    Movement 47
    Participation 2, 18
    Socialisation 17
    Struggles 55
Poona Pact 70, 72
Positivism 4–6, 23, 27, 158
Post-structuralism 30
Prague School of Structuralism 30
Prarthana Samaj 64
Premchand Munshi 8, 10, 20, 79, 85, 86, 87, 88, 90, 92, 93, 94, 99, 100, 135, 160
Progressive Writer's Association 108
Propp, Vladimir 31
Proselytization Movement 62
Prostitution 94
Protection of Civil Rights 55
Protestant Reformation 64
Provincial Government 71

Radical Movements 100
Rajah, M.C. 103, 122
Ram, Babu Jagjivan 123, 127
Ram, Kanshi 121, 146
Ramabai, Pandita 3, 19
Ranade, Mahadeo Govind 64
Rational Criticism 39
Rationalism 25
Ravidas 3, 19, 76, 85, 130, 155, 159
    Jayanti 125–26
Realism 86
Reformative Movement 61–62, 84, 101
Religious Revival 64
Renaissance 38
Representative Studies 8
Republican Party of India 3, 20, 73, 102, 126–27, 137, 145
Reservation Quota 151
Rightist Literature 79
Romanticism 39
Round Table Conferences 70–71, 83
Russian Formalism 30–31

Sanskritisation Movement 62, 66–67

Saraswati, Dayanand 65
Satnami Movement 79
Satyagraha 58
SC and ST (Prevention of Atrocities) Act 152
Scheduled Castes Federation 3, 20, 73
Secular Movements 62, 68
Self Respect Movements 65
Self-Awareness 14
Shah, Ghanshyam 58, 59, 61, 147
Shankaranand 79
Sharma, Ram Vilas 108
Sharma, Satish Kumar 65
Shklovski, Victor 30
Simon Commission 52, 54, 70–71
Singh, Malkhan 8, 10, 131, 132
Singh, Shyoraj 92, 100
SNDA Yogam 67
Social Movement 58–60
Socialist Party 126–27
Socio-Aesthetic Unity 33
Socio-Cultural Structure 76, 84
Socio-Economic Exploitation 48
Sociological
    Literary Criticism 6, 33, 158
    Relevance 35
Sociology of Literature 23, 35, 41
Srinivas, M.N. 66, 71
Structuralism 4, 5, 31–33, 158
Structuration-Destructuration Process 32
Struggle against Oppression 48, 55
Subjective Understanding 56

Tagore, Rabindranath 135
Taine, Hippolyte Adolph 28
Tamil Nadu 66, 68, 146
Temple Entry 100
Theory of
    Idea 23–24
    Justice 15
    Knowledge 25
    Literary 41
Traditional Values 59
Tukaram, Maratha-Kunbi 44

Untouchability 65, 94–95, 107
    Offence Act 55, 74
    Problems of 86
    Conference 84
Uttar Pradesh 45, 68, 146

Varna System 69, 74, 91, 95, 100
Vivekanand, Swami 65

Weldon, T.D. 57
Widow Re-marriage 94
Wilkinson, Paul 60
Williams, Raymond 21, 22, 27, 38, 39, 40, 41

Yadvendu, Bhagwandas 47

Zamindari System 95
Zelliot, Eleanor 43, 73